I D E A S
E X E C U T I O N
R E S U L T S

Andrea Syverson
MARKETING   STRATEGIST

(719) 495-2354
Fax (719) 495-1040

IER PARTNERS
8995 S. Blue Sage Circle
Black Forest, CO 80908

asyverson@ierpartners.com

Advance Praise for
BrandAbout

"To read Andrea is to learn with a smile on your face. Her insights into business and life, and her beautiful writing, make *BrandAbout* **deliciously useful reading for anyone in a position of stewardship of a cherished brand.** I'm buying it for our whole team."

—STEVE LEVEEN, founder, Levenger

"Andrea's work is delightfully refreshing. And just right for the tenor of our times. **Her blueprint for a greater sense of play in how we build brands is soulful, constructive, and fun—a truly unique combination.**"

—ELLEN KRESKY, creative director, Ben & Jerry's

"From the opening story to the last word of advice in *BrandAbout* you'll experience Andrea's down-to-earth sensibility, pragmatism rooted in best practices, and keen sense of smart business strategies that all lead to one important thing—raving, loyal customers who come back to you again and again. **Andrea has helped our organization grow a solid brand using the principles outlined in this book.** If you can't get Andrea in person, this is the next best thing. All of her best tips, tools, and "trade secrets" are laid out with clarity and conciseness. You'll discover that Andrea is not only insightful, but that she truly cares that your brand thrives now and long into the future."

—JOHN VITEK, president, Saint Mary's Press

"Andrea Syverson has written a wonderful work that transcends the traditional business book. Drawing on lessons learned from a lifetime of reading and observing, *BrandAbout* **is not only for the serious entrepreneur, but also delivers a meaningful and thoughtful approach to getting the most out of life.** *BrandAbout* has reconfirmed my belief that the first step to creating a business well run is beginning to understand how to lead a life well lived."

—MITCHELL KAPLAN, owner, Books & Books

"Drawing on her vast consulting repertoire and many life adventures, **Andrea creates playful anecdotes to brilliantly share 10 simple brand lessons to drive customer loyalty.** *BrandAbout* is not another stuffy business book, but an entertaining read with many applicable ideas about marketing and life. Having been fortunate enough to work with Andrea, I know first hand the value of her lessons."

—LAURA BRADY, CEO, Medical Positioning, Inc.

"Having worked with Andrea for over 15 years I was delighted to learn she was writing a book to distill her proven and extensive knowledge of brands and branding. *BrandAbout* **is very a readable, but more importantly a very usable book that provides a road map with lots of specific ideas for building a strong and recognizable brand.** I highly recommend this book for entrepreneurs, seasoned marketers, and anyone searching for demonstrated best practices to establish an identifiable brand."

—JON MEDVED, former CEO of Current, Inc.,
Walter Drake, and CHEFS

"Beginning with the introduction, and continuing in every chapter, it is clear **Andrea Syverson's** *BrandAbout* **is not a conventional business book. She brings a soulful quality to something that is often justly criticized for having none.** Brands often die because they are thought to be static. Successful brands and brand managers understand that businesses, and the brands that define them, need to evolve. If you think you don't have a brand, think again. In today's crowded marketplace having a well-defined, evolving brand may be your key to survival and success. **This book will help you to better understand the importance of your brand and the critical relationship between brands and merchandising. Reading Andrea's book will inspire you to look at your brand with fresh eyes and will help distinguish your brand in the marketplace. A must read.**"

—BOB ALLEN, interim president/CEO,
Direct Marketing Association, and
former president/CEO, Vermont Country Store

BrandAbout

A Seriously Playful Approach
for Passionate Brand-Builders
and Merchants

ANDREA SYVERSON

PMP

Paramount Market Publishing, Inc.

Paramount Market Publishing, Inc.
950 Danby Road, Suite 136
Ithaca, NY 14850
www.paramountbooks.com
Telephone: 607-275-8100; 888-787-8100   Facsimile: 607-275-8101

Publisher: James Madden
Editorial Director: Doris Walsh

Cataloging in Publication Data available
ISBN-10: 0-9819869-2-7 | ISBN-13: 978-0-9819869-2-0

To my dad,
who taught me the importance of work
and
To my husband,
who showed me the importance of play

Contents

With Gratitude

I ECHO Alfred Painter's belief that "saying thank you is more than good manners. It is good spirituality." Practicing gratitude is how I try to live my life. I have many people to thank in relation to this book and I do so with a deeply grateful heart.

I thank Doris Walsh for befriending me as an author and her wise and gentle mentoring of *BrandAbout.* She was my professional and serene hand-holder in this project.

One of the joys of writing this book has been reconnecting with some of my mentors and reflecting on how many people have taken me under their wing, graciously sharing their life and business wisdom with me. Many of these mentors taught me important practices outside of their areas of expertise simply through how they live their lives. I name several of them in this book, but many, many others are named only in my heart. They go back to my parochial grade school days. I thank them all.

I am indebted to my writerly friends who were on- and off-the-page encouragers of this endeavor and quick to help whenever I called upon them. Deep appreciation to Mim Harrison, Patty Dowd Schmitz and Nancy Brummett for their brilliant acumen and friendship.

I am also grateful to my non-writerly but ever loving family and friends who were my constant cheerleaders as this book was coming together. As I said to them over the book-soaked holidays, they were like nourishing bread to me. Thank you for walking alongside of me (quite literally in some cases!), for praying me through this process and for believing in me! You buoyed me.

BrandAbout is in some ways a collection of my 25+ years of practical, in-the-trenches experience. When my husband and I launched IER Partners twelve years ago, we never dreamed our individual business lives would intersect as they did and we would have had such a life-enhancing and rewarding career. The best part of our business is the number of clients who have become our friends outside the workplace.

Many times when I work with companies, I become their brand cheerleader, applauding them in their new directions, reassuring them of their new undertakings. As I interviewed many of them for this book, the tables turned and they became mine. I am grateful to all my clients these past twelve years who have invited me into their brands and allowed me to practice these BrandAbout exercises.

Back in the 1970s when I was still a little girl, my dad used to say that "a woman with a good head on her shoulders would go far in business." I never knew exactly what he meant by that back then, but I hope I've made him proud. I thank both my parents for the sacrifices they made on my behalf, for their loving parenting and for the best gift of all—their faith. Who could ask for more?

And, to Dean, my dear playologist, business partner, and soul mate. You make it all fun.

Lord, I save my most profound thanks for You.

Introduction

I HAD NO IDEA how consequential a three-week, "honeymoon before the wedding" trip to Australia 20 years ago was going to be on my career. I had just uprooted my big-city life in Miami a few months earlier to follow my heart and move out West to be with a rugged but non-smoking "Marlboro Man" of sorts. Soon after unpacking my bags in the Rocky Mountains, Dean had convinced me to spend three weeks playing in Australia and exploring this beautiful country in a camper van and then a sailboat with our very last dollars (as twentysomethings we had not accumulated many). If I tallied up all the time I had spent playing in my 27 years, I'm not sure it would have totaled three weeks. I didn't specialize in play. My nose was often in a book, and because of that, my three younger, more playful sisters didn't always think I was much fun. Three weeks playing? That alone felt almost sinful. And a honeymoon before we were married? That *was* definitely sinful. None of this fazed unconventional Dean. We packed our bags and took off for the land down under and it occurred to me that ours would be an unorthodox marriage and life together.

The Aussies are an independent and unpretentious people quite fond of many things, including all things outdoorsy from tramping to sailing; active participants in all sorts of outback terrain from beautiful coastlines to rainforests to mountains; and quite proud of their many native products and brands like Fosters beer and Penfolds wine, Vegemite, Quiksilver and Billabong surf gear and of course, the Driza-Bone oilskin coats. But it was the aboriginal practice of walkabouts that most resonated with me—a wandering, exploratory, nonlinear but quite insightful process of self discovery.

While the source is unknown, the best definition I've found is this one from *gonewalkabout.com:* "The idea is that a person can get so caught up in one's work, obligations and duties that the truly important parts of one's self become lost. From there it is a downward spiral as one gets farther and farther from the true self. A crisis situation usually develops that awakens the wayward to the absent true self. It is at this time that one must go on walkabout. All possessions are left behind (except for essential items) and one starts walking. Metaphorically speaking, the journey goes on until you meet yourself. Once you find yourself, you sit down and have a long talk about what one has learned, felt and done in each other's absence. One talks until there is nothing left to say— the truly important things cannot be said. If one is lucky, after everything has been said and unsaid, one looks up and sees only one person instead of the previous two."

A few years ago, I realized that more and more of the strategic branding and merchandising work I was doing involved helping clients look up and out and around their brands and product lines by facilitating significant confrontations and conversations about their past, present, and future. So I've called my process a BrandAbout because it involves looking up and out and around. It is a "business walkabout" of sorts, a pause in the daily and weekly hubbub to stop and get not only a sense of how the brand and all its components are evolving, but also time to think about any course corrections that might be warranted. This circumambulation can take many forms but most often it's an inside-out process. And it's almost always transforming.

By "inside out" I mean a couple of things. BrandAbout is an organic process, not a formulaic, one-size-fits-all program. And while I bring in learning and experiences from many other smart branding brains, there is nothing textbook about my approach. It always begins with the "group genius" inside the organization. I provide the "out" lens as an unbiased but experienced practitioner with antennae in several industries, customer segments, and product categories. It always involves all of us rolling up our sleeves together and turning things upside down and inside out to see what we might see differently. It is quite an adventurous sojourn. We have a destination in mind, but we are wide open to the routes and side trips we might take. We are travelers, not tourists.

In my personal life, I am drawn to the subjects of spirituality, simplicity, creativity, and writing. I study these disciplines as much as I immerse myself in branding and merchandising. I find that principles from one of these fields often intersect with one another and my life becomes a Venn diagram (remember those three interlocking circles?) where each discipline informs and enlivens the other.

For example, I am presently and joyfully in the thick of an eight-book series on the topics of the ancient Christian practices edited by Phyllis Tickle. Not at all business related but as I am reading Brian McLaren's understandings of the term "practices," I realize that this is what I am doing in the business world with my clients. "Practices are about life, about training ourselves to become the kinds of people who have eyes and actually see, and who have ears and actually hear, and so experience . . . not just survival but Life, capitalized and modified by insufficient adjectives such as *real, abundant, examined, conscious, worth living and good.* Spiritual practices are ways of becoming awake and staying awake," writes McLaren. I write a big bold YES!!! to McLaren in the book's margins with several exclamation points, hoping he'll feel my agreement with him all the way back in Maryland where he lives and writes and pastors.

But my highly enthusiastic YES!!! to McLaren is also because my antennae connect this definition to what I am doing in the business world. I write a similar YES!!! to Anne Lamott when she discusses writing practices in *Bird by Bird: Some Instructions on Writing and Life,* and to Matthew Crawford when he writes about the glory of being immersed soulfully in your work in his book, *Shop Class as Soulcraft.* See how my readabout tendencies have taken on desultory BrandAbout characteristics?

So, BrandAbout is really all about a series of practices that are life-giving to brands and the people who create them. They are verbs. They are action-specific. They are reminders to do the things you know you want to do—the things that fill your brand's soul. To play. To be. To listen. To conduct. To dare. To herald. To craft. To reveal. To kindle. To integrate.

May this book inspire you and be similar to the experience the folks at LEGO create with their products—"Fun, but hard fun!"

1

Play in the Brand

DESPITE BEING AN AVID READER, I rarely take time to reread books. I am always hungry to feast on the next selection from my "library of candidates" that await me on my home shelves and on my Kindle, as well as those yet to be purchased, downloaded, or even written by my favorite authors. However, there is one book that I have read several times over. It is a gentle reminder of a practice that helps me in all aspects of my life. Richard A. Swenson, M.D., physician-futurist, wrote a constructive and thoughtful book called *Margin*. "Margin" is the term he uses that describes the "space between our load and our limits and is related to our reserves and resilience. It is a buffer, a leeway, a gap; the place we go to heal, to relate, to reflect, to recharge our batteries, to focus on the things that matter most." I think of his book as one giant permission slip. The concept of margin is like the "white spaces" between the lines of these sentences and around the pages that enable the words to breathe more freely and the reader to comprehend them better. Dr. Swenson prescribes many things for creating more margin, but the one I remember most is to build in "downtime" for rest and reflection. I try to practice margin.

Just like people, brands need space to breathe and time to recharge. When they are not properly cared for, brands can become stale, old, tired, and even snarky. Not good! Brands need leaders that understand margin is a necessity, not a luxury, that enables everyone in the company to step back, take a look with fresh eyes, and reexamine whether the brand is being true to its soul.

As a creative branding strategist, I spend a lot of time trying to help my clients create enough margin to have fun with their brands. I had to learn this lesson myself. English author John Ruskin knows this to be true. He writes: "In order that people may be happy in their work, these three things are needed: They must be fit for it. They must not do too much of it. And they must have a sense of success in it."

Airplanes have become one of my favorite places to embrace margin. Usually I am exhausted after long days with my clients. I do not use my plane time for more work, as efficient as that may be; rather, I treat those two-to-four uninterruptible hours as gifts of time. While others around me are busy on their laptops, I like to indulge in my next book or leaf through a stack of magazines. On one flight back from Chicago, I was immersed in Dr. Stuart Brown's book, *Play: How it Shapes the Brain, Opens the Imagination and Invigorates the Soul.* I had been doing quite a bit of research on the importance of play and the necessity of stepping back, taking time-outs, and the need for creating reflective time and space in our highly reactive culture.

There on page 127, under my dim overhead plane light, I read these words: "The quality that work and play have in common is creativity. In both we are building our world, creating new relationships, neural connections, objects. At their best, play and work, when integrated, make sense of our world and our selves. Most importantly, true play that comes from our own inner needs and desires is the only path to finding lasting joy and satisfaction in our work. In the long run, work does not work without play."

While I thought I understood the concept and necessity of

margin quite well, I had never thought about how critical play is to work. I kept reading: "Play is nature's greatest tool for creating new neural networks and for reconciling cognitive difficulties. The abilities to make new patterns, find the unusual among the common and spark curiosity and alert observation are all fostered by being in a state of play. When we play, dilemmas and challenges will naturally filter through the unconscious mind and work themselves out. It is not at all uncommon for people to come back not only re-energized but also with fresh ideas for work."

Like many of my Type A friends and colleagues, I was raised to think of play as a reward *only* after all the work was done. To play first would be irresponsible. "Work first, play later" was no doubt how my parents were raised and how their parents' parents raised them. Thanks to years of being the overly responsible eldest child, a strict but loving Catholic upbringing, and 18 years of serious parochial schooling, I never thought of play as integral to work. Dr. Brown changed my mind. Work does not work without play. Work does not work without play. Work does not work without play. I feel I must write this sentence on my adult blackboard several thousand times.

I have come to believe that all brands need more play time. It is philosopher Martin Buber who reminds us, "Play is the exultation of the possible." I often give my clients permission slips to "play in their brands" in various ways. I am their gentle "nudge", their brand whisperer, their creative provocateur, their imaginative "possibilitizer." I tease them with a visual reminder of play—plastic shovels that we used in the sandboxes of our childhoods. I encourage them to conduct a BrandAbout review of their businesses. Look up, look out, look all around you! Live in the margins of your brand for awhile and see what happens!

While reflecting on this in Frontier's seat 4C, my own neural connection happened: I realized I married a playologist. A playologist is not a playboy. It is a word I created (with poetic license!)

to describe someone who delights in the adventure of play, prioritizes it, and treats it with career-like focus and intentionality. I was rather startled by this discovery because my husband is a man I know well. Dean and I have shared life together for almost two decades and because we have worked side-by-side professionally for more than 12 years, we probably have spent more time together than most retired couples. We live, work, and play together. Despite all this interaction, until I read Stuart's words, I never realized that all the play Dean orchestrates in our life actually contributes greatly to the success of our work. Dean already had an innate understanding that work does not work without play.

I am more of a workologist. Some aspects of being a workologist have served me well, but as I reflect back over both my marriage and my career, I see that it is my husband's playologist tendencies that have added the necessary white spaces to my life. I believe his playologist role has contributed more to our business success than my workologist tendencies. It has always been my husband who has lured me away from my desk to see new lands (Australia, New Zealand, Belize, Tonga, Fiji, the Caribbean, Italy, Canada, Switzerland, Mexico and all sorts of nooks and crannies in the U.S.), to learn new skills (downhill and cross-country skiing, sailing, snowmobiling, adventure biking, kayaking, motorcycling, canoeing), and to experience new cultures, places, and foods, all while handling a full load of client projects. We literally extract ourselves from our work schedules (there's always more to do!) and make play a priority. I used to think of him as outdoorsy and myself as indoorsy, but then I realized that location wasn't really the issue. It was more about our differing needs for relaxation (his being active, mine being passive) and, even more so, our differing mindset about time off and time away that set us apart. I needed a permission slip. Dean didn't.

Dean just takes it as fact that playing is a big part of life. He resonates with the Jeep campaign that touted: *Work Hard. Play Harder.* As the Chief Playologist in our household, every season has planned play, no matter what our workload. From simple weekend camping trips or motorcycle rides in our home state of Colorado, to six-week-long island adventures in the South Pacific, this variety of short and long play adventures may have changed over the years, but they always have been viewed as a necessary part of our lives. We often include our friends in our "play dates" and the richness of our experiences together have given us countless memories as well as acted as sabbaticals for our souls, our marriage, and our business.

I realized that the role of play in my life has been instrumental in my role of strategic business advisor to my clients. I can see things about their brands and products and customers with a clear lens, a clear mind, and a clear heart. I am not enmeshed in corporate political issues or worn down by sacred cows or imprisoned by a title or a level or even a department. Time away and apart from their daily business issues gives me an uncluttered and unbiased view. The hours I've logged on the ocean or in the mountains or in culturally different settings and in testing my own personal limits have given me the focus, the margin, the creativity, and the confidence to be bold with my strategic recommendations.

Serious play

When I am working with my clients, I often experience the joy of "aha!" moments when together we resolve problems or set visions or create new products or programs. We are connected by a shared sense of mission; we bring all we have to the task at hand; we experience what Professor Mihaly Csikszentmihalyi coined as "flow." He describes it as "a state of concentration so focused that it amounts to absolute absorption in an activity."

In an interview in *Wired* magazine, Csikszentmihalyi elaborates: "Flow is being involved in an activity for its own sake. The ego falls away. Time flies. Your whole being is involved and you're using your skills to the utmost." Flow is a lot like deep play.

Poet, essayist and naturalist Diane Ackerman wrote a treatise on this same subject and called it *Deep Play*. Ackerman's definition of deep play adorns the cover of her book: "(1.) A state of unselfconscious engagement with our surroundings. (2.) An exalted zone of transcendence over time and (3.) A state of optimal creative capacity."

She writes, "Deep play has been such an important part of my life. Opportunities for deep play abound. In its thrall we become ideal versions of ourselves. We long for its heights, which some people often visit and others must learn to find, but everyone experiences as replenishing." For Ackerman, deep play makes her "deciduously happy." She believes that "Deep play allows one to feel quintessentially alive, heartbeat by heartbeat, in the eternal present. The here and now becomes a pop-up storybook, full of surprises, in which everything looms. It returns us to the openness of childhood."

Did you know that there is a National Institute for Play? Yes, for grown-ups and for organizations! Founded by a medical doctor and researcher, its sole purpose is to "bring the unrealized knowledge, practices and benefits of play into public life," and to teach brands "how to do the work of their organizations in a play state."

What is your brand's play state?

There are indeed companies that operate their organizations in a play state and I've had the honor of working with a few of them. They take an intentional approach to creating a fun working environment for both employees and customers. Companies like Southwest, Ben & Jerry's, Jim Beam, Chipotle, and LEGO all know that serious play leads to happy productive workers and to brands that customers enjoy doing business with.

I attend a biannual conference at Calvin College that is unlike most of my business conferences. It is playful in both its name, "Festival of Faith and Writing," and its personality. "Festival" booths are set up on the campus to encourage lingering, with both fellow attendees and published authors. People are listening to and learning from one another in a relaxed and congenial atmosphere. It is indeed a celebration and a far cry from typical business conventions where I see people on their Blackberries all day communicating with their home offices while sitting through boring PowerPoint presentations, calling it educational (and waiting until the free drinks kick in).

We need more true playfulness in our brand days. Mark Twain once wrote: "Work and play are words used to describe the same thing under differing conditions." I'll never forget an unconventional training program I experienced when I worked at Current, Inc., a company that in its heyday was the first to sell greeting cards and accessories like gift wrap by mail. Our industry was called "social expression," that is, it consisted of products that help you say all the right things in all the right ways. Cards and what they communicated were our bread and butter. Nancy Brummett, then manager of Creative Services, came up with an artful way to teach those of us not in her department exactly what they did.

Here's her story: "The day I heard someone giving a tour of our department say, 'And these are the people who write the ditties for the greeting cards,' I knew we had some serious internal image-building to do. Our department, Creative Services, actually included editorial copywriters and editors, graphic designers, and advertising copywriters. Each product developed by the company had to be touched by each of these areas before it could be completed. The creativity we put into each product was key to its ultimate sales success. But, evidently, who knew?

"The solution was to offer one day of cross-training to anyone in the company who wanted to learn more about what we did in Creative Services. We called the day 'Creative Pursuits,' and participants moved from station to station developing their prototype product during the day. At each station, they would complete a different task and learn some 'Trivial Pursuit' type facts about each area of our department. At the end of the day they knew we were more than the 'ditty writers,' and they enjoyed themselves as well. The program enjoyed positive reviews over a period of several months."

I still remember how fun that day was and how much I learned by "doing" my own product. A playful day with long-lasting repercussions!

Go play outside!

I joke with my mom that her three favorite words when we were growing up were "Go play outside!" As four daughters being raised in New Jersey in the 1960s, we heard those words all summer long. Like the Springsteen song, "our screen door slammed" behind us in the early morning and we were out all day until we were called back in for dinner. In between we played kickball, created mud pie bakeries, rode our banana-seat bikes to the creek, dreamed up neighborhood carnivals, and just generally had no adult supervision for hours on end. (Maybe I did play for more than three weeks after all!) These were the days before scheduled play dates.

Sometimes, in our work places, the only way things get done is if they are scheduled. So perhaps it's time to get out. Out of your cubicle. Out of your home office. Out of your company's group think. Out of your industry's bigger group think. Just get out. It's time to get sideways. You'll be amazed at what a little "playing outside" can do to rattle your inside perspectives. So, like my mother, I encourage brands to "go play outside!"

One of my clients didn't need any prompting at all. Over the last 36 years, entrepreneurs Thom and Joani Schultz have built an impressive business called Group, that comes alongside people in ministry and provides them with innovative resources. Joani is the chief creative officer at Group. She knows that good things happen when she plays outside. "I treasure time to break out of the norm. Getting away from the daily routine opens up new ways to experience the world. Travel jolts me into making connections I would otherwise never make. (I'm crazy because I even love long flights—and getting in the "zone"!) Travel rejuvenates me! I love immersing myself into other cultures—the sounds, tastes, sights, textures, and smells. Our love of adventure travel and heart for serving others inspired us to add a new experiential aspect to our company called Lifetree Adventures. I like to say it's Indiana Jones meets Mother Teresa!" Playing outside can be productive in many ways.

As a merchant at heart, I like to connect the dots when I see new product innovation and try to unravel where the new thinking came from. Did a stop at the liquor store or a fun evening out at a hip happy hour spot inspire the new bubble bath packaged in the shape of a wine bottle? Did the upside-down ketchup bottle in the refrigerator door inspire Target's new color-coded prescription bottles? I will never know for sure, but I do know that these product development designers and creators weren't simply looking at their companies' previous models and trying to create more of the same. They got out. They looked up. They looked down. They looked sideways. They connected dots from outside their industry and brought that thinking into their own in revolutionary new ways.

John Le Carré wrote: "A desk is a dangerous place from which to watch the world." I know this to be true because I experienced it first-hand in my days of working as a merchant at Current, Inc. When the company was founded in 1950, the places a customer could buy greeting cards were limited. As time went on, this product category became more readily available at grocery stores and discount stores and was even showing up in unexpected places like craft stores, car washes, and airport gift shops. By the early 1990s, cards were available everywhere.

The management team at Current knew that the company's competition was changing and understood this intellectually, but hadn't really experienced it. As men, they rarely sent cards themselves but relied on their stay-at-home wives who did the shopping and the card-buying and sending. Most of my female colleagues knew this not only intellectually, but quite experientially as we made trips to places like Target, Walmart, Safeway, and Hobby Lobby on a weekly basis for our households. We saw the card and holiday accessories aisles growing; we appreciated the convenience of throwing a greeting card in our shopping baskets. As is true for many companies, the management team did not represent the socio-demographic of the company's customer base (mid-America moms with middle incomes). A brand field trip for the executive team would have proved quite valuable to get an updated glimpse into the product category and also experience "a day in the life" of their average busy mom customer.

This example from Current, Inc. is not unusual. What keeps brand leaders from experiencing their brands through the lens of their customers? Busyness? Corporate arrogance? Lack of margin? Lack of scheduled play dates? All of the above?

Well, let's get up and take a stroll around a few industries and window shop into their brands. Let's rediscover the fine art of rambling around via these pages and see if we can learn a few things that we can bring back to our tasks at hand.

Strolling for inspiration

For total freedom and independence (not to mention adventure and fun!), there's nothing like a stop at the local Harley-Davidson dealer to find inspiration. I have always learned a great deal from this brand and I continue to admire its gutsy moves. For years, innovative business thinkers like Tom Peters, Seth Godin, and Mary Lou Quinlan have been advising companies across many spectrums to take women seriously. Harley is one that does. While presently women account for just 12 percent of its sales, Harley believes that number has nowhere to go but up. It isn't waiting passively. A few years ago it started "Garage Parties"—an unusual but contemporary and ingenious twist on Tupperware parties. Harley dedicates a significant part of its website to these events and invites women only to these get-togethers which "offer fun, basic instruction for non-riders who have little—or even no—prior knowledge of motorcycles." And Harley declared May, 2010 the first-ever Women Riders Month, a chance to "honor all the women who enjoy the freedom and adventure found in taking control of their own handlebars."

It also launched a promotion that gives away Harley rings —designed by Karen Davidson, great-granddaughter of one of the company's founders—to women who buy a new bike and graduate from the Rider's Edge training program. The ring, inscribed "Live to Ride. Ride to Live," while fashionable in its own right, is also a great symbol of conquering fear and a proud badge of independence. These parties plant dreams and help women who want to own their own bike but feel a bit intimidated conquer that fear. Brilliant marketing: plant dreams and quell fears.

Next stop on our window-shopping tour is your favorite bookseller or discount store or practically *wherever* books are sold because that is just where you'll find whatever book everyone is buzzing about. These days books find their readers in the strangest of places! Whether it's the surprise best-selling series about vampires, *The Twilight* sagas, or a Christian fable, *The Shack,* or the event-driven books based on the latest political event, even non-readers can't miss these sensations. J.K. Rowling's last Harry Potter book (and all others!) was both a marketer's dream and a reader's dream. Even if you are not a fan, you couldn't have missed the pre-selling frenzy of *Harry Potter and the Deathly Hallows.* It was extraordinary. Pajama parties at midnight were held at many local independent bookstores and sales records were set at online retailers, bookstores, as well as other non-traditional outlets. It seemed as if the whole world was waiting for Harry.

The lovely, ultra-luxe Gorsuch ski-clothing company knows a bit about this provocative technique. In the middle of last year's record-breaking hot Colorado summer, it emailed a "Coming Soon" catalog teaser message. Visions of Vail started dancing in my head and I realized that ski season was only 120 days away! It not only planted dreams, but created anticipation too.

Now, let's go into Best Buy. There in the midst of the shelves and displays we see branded experts (vendor reps) from the various technology companies like Dell and HP just walking around helping and selling people on their particular products. Real live highly trained people who provide relevant customer service to potential customers in real time. "Mingling" as an intentional business strategy. Vendors as partners. Vendors making friends with customers.

Another twist on this is the Apple Store Genius Bar. Apple employees are on a mission to "answer all your technical questions, troubleshoot problems and explain it all in a language that's easy to understand." Now that is *real* service!

Brands like L.L.Bean, Nordstrom, The Ritz-Carlton, Levenger, Garmin and a few others raise the bar. Their personnel make an art out of customer service. It's a true pleasure to do business with them. They can answer most customer questions and they also love what they do. It shows.

Now, let's take a break and watch a few commercials. Even if you are a TiVo addict, you can't have missed the quirky characters at Aflac and Geico over the last few years. Quacking ducks. Quirky cavemen. Serious products and services not taking themselves too seriously. Campaigns that won awards and more importantly, produced results.

Sometimes brands can take themselves too seriously. If yours suffers from this malady, how can you let go and give up some control? Kelly Mooney, in her book, *The Open Brand,* asks the question, "Are you dangerously closed?" Her O.P.E.N. acronym stands for being open, personal, engaging, and networked—a short cut for what really matters to customers these days. So, how can your brand open up? Be more relevant? Be more enticing? Maybe even poke a little fun at yourself?

The wine industry is a great example of one that has humbled itself over recent years. The snooty factor still exists but the fun factor has sold a great deal more wine. Labels like Mad Housewife or Mommy's Time Out, 7 Deadly Zins, or even Harley-Davidson's custom-labeled V-Twin Zin spark sales and conversations.

Getting a bit hungry? Let's go into Whole Foods. Here, grocery shopping is no longer a dreaded chore. Walking into the store is like walking into a local farmer's market at peak season, only to turn the corner and be in a beautiful flower shop, and then turn around again and you're at your favorite deli, cheese bar, and olive bar all-in-one. They've mastered the concept of "treasure hunt," first documented by Michael J. Silverstein in a book of the same name while adding the sensory delight of feasting on samples of exotic and organic foods. Even your everyday staples seem somehow elevated here. Your shopping cart becomes a picnic basket, a gourmet treasure chest waiting to be placed in perfect, delectable rows on display in your home pantry.

Anthropologie also masters the art of treasure hunting. It offers a sophisticated flea market of artsy finds that encourage the joy of discovery, especially in its store designs. You turn around and see china plates and funky fashions and then turn sideways to see eclectic books and vintage signs. It encourages peripatetic meanderings.

Back to the desk. Hopefully this little field trip "on paper" inspired your soul and gave you some outside-in thinking for whatever you might be working on next. I encourage you to take a pause from your daily routine and go on your own treasure hunt and see what you might discover! What I like about brand field trips are all the unexpected insights that arise and the questions that get provoked. Traveling is like that. As Martin Buber reminds us: "All journeys have secret destinations of which the traveler is unaware."

The fine art of moodling

Have you ever *moodled?* College kids may have moodled at Moodle.org, a website for open-source community-based tools for learning. But long before this website, I learned this term from Brenda Ueland, an author and creativity encourager. Moodling is one of my favorite words. She writes, "So you see, imagination needs moodling—long, inefficient, happy idling, dawdling and puttering." As a brand leader, moodling would have you pondering questions like these after our above-mentioned field trip.

After the Harley-Davidson dealership visit:

How can your company plant dreams and quell fears with your brand? Do you know your customers well enough to know what their fears are?

After the bookstore visit:

Are your customers waiting for your next installment? Have you created desire? A teaser campaign of sorts? Have you built demand in unconventional ways?

After popping into Best Buy:

Do you have people who are highly trained on your product intricacies *and* passionate (not just clock-watchers) about assisting your customers? Do they care? Are they the most important hires in your company? Do they have "genius status" in your company?

After viewing the Aflac and Geico commercials:

Is there room for any brand fun within your brand boundaries? Have you spent time thinking about eye-catching labels or names or packaging for your products?

After the Whole Foods excursion:

Does your brand make the ordinary extraordinary? Do you actively pull your customers into your products through any kind of sampling program? Can your customers experience the "thrill of wandering" throughout your store or catalog or website?

Like pausing and playing, moodling often gets pushed out of our schedules. But it is in the moodles that things can occur to us. Things like changes to our present structures (either people or processes), product and/or system enhancements, or even ways to improve our own customer experiences based on things we observe outside our own categories. Taking time to write, record, and process the nuanced field notes from our observations is an important step to clarifying what action to take. Nike builds on this idea and actually has customers assigned as "Field Report-

ers" as part of its brand strategy. These young women share their moodles (blogs, interviews with athletes, and exercise tips) online and help Nike stay an O.P.E.N. brand.

Other ways to moodle include scheduling what Julia Cameron calls "Artist's Dates." These are trips or activities meant only to fill your soul, to charge your batteries. Unlike the above mentioned play dates for your brand, these play dates are just for you. Cameron advocates making a list of varying types of activities that would feed your soul—from ideas that would take 15 minutes (i.e., strolling through a gourmet shop if you like to cook) to longer two-to-three hour outings (i.e., taking in a concert, movie, or play). They do not need to cost money or take a lot of time. She encourages us to fit in one artist date a week. I share this idea with my clients and we take the time right then and there to make these lists. I check in with them at a later date and encourage them to share their stories about these mini adventures. It is a small way to start adding margin to our lives. None have ever told me they regretted their Artist Dates.

Inc. magazine interviewed Bobbi Brown, founder and CEO of Bobbi Brown Cosmetics: "I believe it's important to recharge your batteries and that means getting out of the office from time to time. Go take a walk. Better yet, take a day off or even a week off, if you can manage it. It will actually help you do your job better. Great decisions aren't made sitting in an office."

Matt Frederick—creative director at 5.11 Tactical, a company specializing in clothing that enhances the safety, accuracy, speed, and performance of law enforcement, military, and firefighting professionals—moodles, although it might not be the exact word he uses. Here's what he told me: "I am a creative at heart, and always have new and unique projects in the works. Often, work as a creative director has more to do with deadlines and production than it has to do with creativity. When things get really crazy at the office I start looking for new or existing projects to tackle in my own time, however limited that can be. These 'escapes' from everyday work and production are essential. Recently that's been the rediscovery of intaglio printmaking and it's been a great learning experience, including a two-week sabbatical in the middle of nowhere, Nevada. Can't stop learning. Ultimately it all rolls together into who I am: a creative—at work and at play."

Moodling can happen within your traditional business venues. I remember Joan Litle, a brilliant merchandiser and mentor of mine, telling me years ago that she learned from Chuck Williams (founder of Williams-Sonoma) to take in trade shows in reverse. To yes, walk around it one way but then do it all over in the opposite direction. "You'd be amazed what you see the second time around that you missed the first!" she advised. I know this to be true. Moodling may be inefficient from a time-motion perspective, but from a creativity-enhancing perspective, it's one of the best things you can do. I wonder what else we would learn about our brands if we "toured" them in reverse!

John Vitek, president of Saint Mary's Press, an innovative curriculum publisher headquartered in Minnesota, spent some time with his marketing team one summer white water rafting in Colorado as a way to celebrate their recent brand successes. While they would use a different word than moodling to classify the intense thrill of white water rafting, this play date certainly filled their souls, created memories, and energized each team leader. Bev DeGeorge, vice president for mission, shared her reflections on that experience: "Navigating white waters with my colleagues certainly elevated the rules of teamwork to a new level! We yelled; we laughed; we cheered. Our play together forged a bond of camaraderie and shared memories of that day that carried forward long into the days ahead at the workplace. And I think each team member secretly enjoyed watching John and me, up front in the raft, placed there by the team, bearing the brunt of each wave. After experiencing the collective risk and trust inherent in successfully navigating a raft together far away from the office, the days ahead back in a business setting found us better collaborators, communicators, and problem solvers. We were generally just more comfortable being open with each other, trusting each other."

And yes, you can moodle without even leaving your home or office. One of my favorite things to do is to buy five to seven magazines from fields that I normally do not read or study and just page through them. I often do this at airports when I am tired. Sometimes all I do is look at the photos, the headlines, the designs, the type faces, and especially, the ads. I always learn about something I've never been exposed to before and appreciate these new perspectives.

So, be intentional about feeding your soul, not just to make you a stronger, more creative brand leader, but to make you a better you!

Recess time

We know time off is good and necessary, but we just don't take enough of it. Scottish novelist and poet George MacDonald wrote: "Work is not always required. There is such a thing as sacred idleness, the cultivation of which is now fearfully neglected." When is the last time you experienced sacred idleness either in or out of the workplace? We need more brand leaders who recognize the importance of charging batteries, not just for themselves, but for all their employees.

Jeffrey Katzenberg, chief executive of DreamWorks Animation SKG, shared some of his learning lessons on this topic in a *New York Times* interview: "For many years, our studio used to, particularly when we were in the rush of finishing a production, we always would work six-day weeks and sometimes seven, and the burnout factor of that started to become meaningful. So we actually strive, really, really hard today not to work a sixth day, since the quality of work in that sixth day is just not at the same level. Since we're not in the quantity business but the quality business, it's a big difference. So for our 2,000 artists, it's critical to recharge and have outside interests and experience other things. It's like fuel."

In another *New York Times* interview, William D. Green, chairman and CEO of Accenture, the global management consulting firm, shared this: "In our company, usually in the summer, people ask me, 'When are you going on vacation?' Because when I come back from a week's vacation, they know I've had time to think and reflect and have been strategizing about changes and it could be anything. Even my outside board members say, 'When are you taking vacation, Bill?'"

Management consultant Tom Peters is a proponent of "radical sabbaticals." Time away from everything. Time unplugged and unfettered. Time to let your soul catch up with you. I was glad to see that this topic was given some coverage at the 2009 TED (Technology Entertainment Design) Global Conference. TED devotes itself "to ideas worth spreading." Designer Stefan Sagmeister gave a powerful speech on the topic of "The Power of Time Off." He practices what he preaches and takes a year off every seven. He knows that without this break, all his edgy creative work starts to look the same and that is not what his clients pay him to produce. No one told Sagmeister to do this. Knowing he is a journal keeper, I like to think that he came to these thoughts via moodling.

No one told advertising executive Mary Lou Quinlan to take

time off either. A self-professed Type A good girl, Quinlan decided to walk away from her overscheduled life for five weeks. "She then chronicled her experience and those of several other sabbatical-embracers in *Time Off for Good Behavior.* Her sabbatical led her to start a new research company called Just Ask a Woman. Sabbaticals often have life-changing effects.

Marc Benioff, chairman and CEO of Salesforce.com writes in his book, *Behind the Cloud,* about the power of his sabbatical. "My sabbatical was one of the most productive periods of my career; it was certainly one of the most influential. Don't be afraid to take time off when you need it. You could learn something that will change the course of your life, and at the least you will stave off the burnout that plagues so many driven entrepreneurial people."

When Denise Tedaldi was vice president, brand strategy and product innovation for the Medford, Oregon-based gourmet gift company, Harry & David, she was given an eight-week paid sabbatical. When I chatted with Denise, she discussed a few personal and professional aspects of her "heavenly" experience. "I so appreciated that Harry & David, valued its executives that much and understood the need for recharging. Eight weeks is long enough to plan a vocation vacation (many have done this), or an extended trip where you deep dive into the culture of another country, or to really do the charity project that has been tickling your brain. My sabbatical allowed a bit of the above, but also allowed me to spend time with my husband, just to be sure we could get along daily at the point that we might consider retiring! I was nervous! It turned out that we really do like each other, and we had the opportunity to travel without the limits of having to be somewhere on a certain day. It was heavenly! We also rented an apartment in the city and became New Yorkers for three weeks. It was a terrific experience in an 1820's building furnished with antiques and a 4 flight walk-up in the meat packing district. I was ready to move there; my rancher husband not quite so enthusiastic! The other important part of a sabbatical is the team you leave in charge for eight weeks. It really allows the next in command the opportunity to manage your challenges and show their real leadership abilities. It's a great way to build a strong management team."

McDonald's is another long-term believer in sabbaticals. All eligible employees can take an eight-week sabbatical for every ten years of full-time continuous service with the company. It's been reported that some employees are on their fourth time away. That's 32 *extra* weeks off over the course of a 40-year career! Add regular vacation time to that model and you are well over the 10 percent mark of time off per time on the job. Seems like a good work tithe to me.

Work tithe

Some companies really do practice a business version of the spiritual discipline of tithing. That is, they give back to their employees a percentage of time that their employees give them. I love this idea. You've no doubt heard about these places. They have innovation built into their core brand DNA—places like 3M, Google, and Microsoft. Their "work tithes" have proved quite valuable; each of these companies can point directly to products that were created because of these policies.

3M shares its practice on its website:

> "To foster creativity, 3M encourages technical staff members to spend up to 15 percent of their time on projects of their own choosing. Also known as the "bootlegging" policy, the 15 percent rule has been the catalyst for some of 3M's most famous products, such as Scotch Tape and—of course—Post-it Notes."

Google has its famous 20 percent time policy where engineers can take one day a week to work on what they're really passionate about. Google credits Gmail, Google News, Google Talk, Google Sky, and a host of other projects to this policy.

Microsoft's chairman Bill Gates is known for his "Think Weeks" where he takes one or two solitary week retreats (no calls, no email, just a big supply of Diet Orange Crush and white papers from his staff) to simply reflect.

Are there some ways your brand can implement a work tithe?

Play in the Brand Homework

Here are some exercises that will encourage the practice of "playing in the brand." Why not schedule a few play dates and see what happens?

⫸ Playlist permission slip

Let's talk playlists. No, not for your iPod; for your life, for your brand. Make two lists. The first is your personal play list. Write down five or ten potential Artist's Dates that would feed your soul. Try to have different lengths of activities with some that take only a few minutes, to a few that are a couple hours, to ones that are full days. Now schedule at least one of those activities into your next week. Go ahead.Give yourself permission. You need the fuel. And remember what toy inventor Frank Caplan said: "Play has been man's most useful occupation."

The next playlist can be done with your leadership team. Brainstorm five or ten companies or places outside your industry that intrigue you. Divide up the list and go wander and ramble and linger in the margins of these companies. Make it a brand walkabout of your own. Take field notes. Moodle over your discoveries, come back together and share your discoveries to see what sideways thinking can do for you and your brand!

))) Create your own recess

Pretend your company has policies like 3M, Google, and Microsoft. If you were able to take a "work recess" what would you do? Take time to ponder this for both your personal life (a true sabbatical . . . how would you use the time off?) and also for your professional life (what projects would you really like to work on?). Now, like Sagmeister and Quinlan, how might you go about making recess happen for yourself?

))) Brand wanderlust

Take a "WebAbout" tour of several brands' "Play" or "Fun Stuff" or "Experience" tabs on their sites. Explore the activities, the downloads, the photos, the games. Get started with Chipotle, Jim Beam, Ben & Jerry's, and Jeep and then go find others. Have some fun and see if you can connect any of these whimsical dots for your brand experience.

⟫ Plays well with others

Fortune magazine wondered what would happen if two CEOs from its Best Companies list traded places for a day and worked in the trenches of each other's brands. So Kip Tindell, CEO, Container Store and Maxine Clark, CEO, Build-A-Bear, did just that. This creative BrandAbout approach to on-the-job training in different industries was eye-opening for Tindell and Clark and they each discovered innovative practices they could borrow from one another. Why not try doing the same thing in your role? Trade places with someone in an entirely distinct world from yours. Compare notes. See what happens.

2

Be Insatiably Curious

JIM COLLINS, a highly acclaimed author perhaps best known for his book, *Good to Great: Why Some Companies Make the Leap . . . and Others Don't,* uses the term *student* as the first descriptor in his impressive bio. It is only later that you learn about all his degrees. The bio goes on to say that he is "driven by a relentless curiosity." Genuinely humble people impress me. They are rare. It doesn't surprise me that Collins seems to share both humility and a love of learning with Albert Einstein, who said modestly, "I have no special gift. I am only passionately curious."

Would you ever describe yourself first as a student? As passionately curious?

The word "student" conjures up either good or bad memories based on your experiences (or report cards!). People either resonate with Rabbi Abraham Joshua Heschel's philosophy that "The school is a sanctuary . . . learning is a form of worship" or these lines from a Springsteen's "No Surrender":

> *We busted out of class had to get away from those fools*
> *We learned more from a three minute record than we ever*
> *learned in school.*

But luckily, curiosity is not at all about whether you loved or hated formal schooling; it is about having an inquisitive mind. Brand leaders need to be lifelong learners.

A friend, who was further down the marriage journey than I, shared this excellent advice with me soon after Dean and I married. "Be a student of your husband," she said wisely. Despite being quite bookish and an honors student most of my school life, I don't think this would have naturally occurred to me. I took her advice to heart.

Master facilitator Jennifer Brewer of Fierce, Inc., wrote this in her blog, headlined, *What don't you know already?* "How about making it a point to learn something new about someone? Curiosity is a beautiful way of showing someone how much you care about them and to gain new appreciation for them."

Are you curious about your co-workers? How much time have you spent trying to figure out your customers? Your competitors? Is your company passionately curious about the world in which your brand operates?

UK branding expert Colin Bates encourages brands to become learning businesses with this advice: "Continuously improving your brand-led marketing effectiveness is essential to long-term success. The best way to achieve this is to ensure that you take a little time to become a 'learning business' by building learning into your processes."

So, just how do you do that? Perhaps the best example of continuous learning as a practice in corporate culture comes from the global PR firm, Edelman. In their program "Living in Color" the staff is encouraged to immerse themselves not only in their work but also explore all kinds of outside interests. To Edelman, "living in color" means "leading a culturally rich and rewarding life outside of work. It means spending time with your family. It means giving back to your community. It means taking the time to learn about the world around you and your place in it." I believe all brands can and should "live in color" whether they are one-woman entrepreneurial ventures or global franchises.

One of my clients, Compassion International, a global Christian sponsorship ministry, practices living in color in a dramatic way. David Dahlin, executive vice president, explains: "At Compassion International, one of the ways we help employees to live the brand is by taking them overseas to experience our work with children in poverty first hand. Although their day-to-day jobs are in an office building in the United States, the impact that they are having is in the lives of more than one million children living in poverty. One of our brand personality traits is to be authentic. Giving employees an authentic experience of the developing world helps them live the brand of Compassion." This immersion not only deepens the employees' first-hand knowledge of the children's daily living conditions, but enables the employees to interact more meaningfully with the childrens' sponsors. Living in color is a branding practice that has many ripple effects.

In 2009 National Geographic launched a global brand campaign called "Live Curious." David Haslingden, CEO of National Geographic Channels, says "'Live Curious' is at the heart of National Geographic's DNA and the National Geographic brand is one of the most familiar and powerful global brands, transcending borders and cultures." This brand wants to encourage worldwide curiosity. "Live Curious is about explora-

tion, pioneering and questioning, which captures National Geographic's shared spirit," said Rafael Sandor, executive vice president of creative and marketing for the company. Like Lance Armstrong's inspirational "Live Strong" campaign, the idea of "Live Curious" motivates brand leaders both inside and outside the office!

There are many ways to Live Curious

As an artist and writer, Rosie Harris, creator of Gallery Walk of Faith, an interactive creative arts worship experience, is inquisitive by nature. Her creativity is spurred on "by letting what I see, what I know and the circumstances around me collide in my head and fall out on paper or in paragraphs." But recently, Harris became curious about her "mistakes." She shared this: "There's nothing quite like a shipwreck to help us discover that the broken planks can be kickboards. They can save us and float us to a place we never would have thought of going. When a friend encouraged me to 'listen to the errors,' I did. I was in the midst of tearing up old and useless paintings in my studio when I got the inspiration to save pieces of these works of art and create both a unique series of encouraging cards and a life-affirming creative experience for others to share. My old stuff became new again. This principle of deconstructing the old to create something useful and new has captured my life."

What would happen if you became curious about your mistakes?

Steve Leveen, co-founder of Levenger, a company that creates and provides "tools for serious readers," was taught by one of his mentors to "notice what you're noticing." That is, be curious about what you're paying attention to! A life-long learner and one of my mentors, Leveen notices the clever names of rather ordinary products all around him—grocery items, clothes, furniture. "They are springing up all around me," Leveen said. "From "I Can't Believe It's Not Butter to Boyfriend Jackets to Not Your Daughter's Jeans to even our own Levenger No-Room-For-a-Table Table. These names tell it all. They deliver the brand promise right in the product name. Customers get it immediately." Leveen took this learning back to his merchants and marketers and encouraged them to push the envelope more on naming their exclusive products. "Promise me this," he told them, "take more chances on creating more edgy and interesting names."

What would happen if you became more curious about what you were noticing?

Chambers of wonder

How can your brand live more curiously? As Albert Einstein reminds us, "The important thing is not to stop questioning. . . . Never lose a holy curiosity."

When Brother Michael Quirk, FSC became the new president of Christian Brothers Services, a comprehensive benefits firm, he brought with him a holy curiosity. Since he came from an entirely different industry (academia), he was primed to see the company through a new lens. He invited me into the brand and we worked together, gently questioning the ways things were. Quirk told me: "While the company was very well established, the branding process we went through revealed a lot about the company—how we looked at ourselves and how our customers viewed us. We discovered that despite being around for more than 40 years, we made too many assumptions about who we were, and even our best customers weren't fully informed about all our programs and services. This process has energized our company and focused our efforts to engage our current customers at higher levels as well as broadened the company's image in our market. You challenged a company that was set in its ways and helped us become a better company for our customers and our employees."

Sometimes being a learning business means having to unlearn some things, relearn other things, and be open to all the accidental learnings along the way—all the while remaining humble. That is what I believe Einstein meant by holy curiosity.

Dan Allender, president of Mars Hill Graduate School, elaborates a bit more on why some view curiosity as a sacred thing:

"Curiosity is a gift of the Spirit. It loves to be taken as a guest into the chambers of wonder to be humbled and lifted up only to ask, 'Is there more?' The question of what is more is asked either of greed or wonder. If asked out of greed, then nothing will satisfy and there will be no rest – only linear, focused, unrelenting ambition. If what motivates the heart is the delight in wonder, then the desire for more will prompt a complex search that ends up with fascinating connections, interplay, and unity."

Curiosity is indeed all about fascinating connections and interplay—especially as they relate to your customers. Michael Tiernan, now chairman of the board for Boston Proper, spent most of his years as CEO and president of this women's apparel brand being curious about what made his female customer tick. He told me that he still remembers a phrase his father taught him: "You don't change the customer, the customer changes you!" Tiernan reflected on how the brand leaders at Boston Proper are always trying to understand what the customer needs and connecting their offers back to what she wants. "The biggest change is that she is online. Over 60 percent of our business now comes in over the internet. She's asked us to make our navigation easier in certain ways and we've listened. We've responded to her growing interests in travel (with BP Travel) and her desire to stay in shape (with BP Sport). What hasn't changed is her busyness. She values shopping directly. She appreciates the way we edit our selection of clothes with her in mind. Yes, our customer has changed us and we are glad!"

How can you continually tap into your brand's chamber of wonder?

Calling all curious monkeys

Did you grow up reading the adventures of Curious George? That rascal of a monkey that never stopped asking questions? Starting

with their very first book in
1941, authors Hans and Mar-
grey Rey developed George's
signature style of "humor,
adventure, playfulness, and
storytelling." Readers loved
(and continue to love!) this
character. Curious George
went on to sell over 40 million copies and even inspired

an annual event in Boston called Curiosity Day which helps to
celebrate a love of reading and learning. Perhaps brands should
have their own annual Curiosity Days!

"Curiosity is one of the permanent and certain characteristics of a vigorous mind," wrote English author Samuel Johnson.
Many companies are looking for that very aspect of emotional
intelligence when hiring. Adam Bryant writes a "Corner Office"
column in *The New York Times* where he interviews top leaders
on a variety of managerial topics. When he spoke with Best Buy's
CEO, Brian Dunn, the subject of curiosity came up. Dunn believes
it's important to be curious. "I describe it as active learning. And
one of the things I do is set out across our enterprise and look
for ideas, people doing things in ways that are different, doing
things that are important for our future. And it's not just inside
our enterprise; it's outside the enterprise as well."

In that same series, Timberland's CEO Jeffrey Swartz acknowl-
edged that he also seeks out curious people when he hires. Swartz
says: "I ask them questions like "When you're alone by yourself
in a city, what do you do at night? And, if I was going to hang
out with you, what would we do together? What would you show
me? What would you like me to see?" Swartz wants people with
inquisitive souls.

As does Kevin Roberts, CEO of Saatchi & Saatchi, the world's leading creative organization. He was interviewed in a *WSJ.com* webcast about his hiring process. "I look for people who are passionate, restless, love ideas and are inherently curious."

Matt Seiler is CEO of Universal McCann, a global marketing communications company whose tagline is "Curious minds for surprising results." *Adweek* describes it this way: "Seiler has taken the theme of curiosity and made it the core tenet of the agency, going so far as to develop a 'curiosity quotient' to assess new hires. Even the company intranet is now curiosity-themed with a question of the day that is answered the following day. 'Compensation to some extent will now be linked to curiosity,' said Seiler. 'We're fundamentally overhauling the training to insure that new people coming in have a certain level of curiosity and that the people that are here are kept fresh on what being curious is. We define it as open-mindedness that leads to unexpected or surprising results.'" I like that definition.

So, in addition to entertaining children of all ages, perhaps Curious George would have made a great brand leader. His signature style of "humor, adventure, playfulness, and storytelling" would make personnel directors smile.

How can your brand increase the curiosity quotient of its entire culture?

Stretching lessons

Nobel laureate Dr. Arno Penzias tells us another reason why curiosity is so important: "Invention is the product of a creative or curious mind. Innovation is something that changes the life of a customer. It changes the life of the customer in some way, or the world in which the customer experiences things. That's an innovation."

Great things can happen when brand leaders flex their curiosity muscles. I see it all the time. Here are a few BrandAbout examples of companies that are stretching their muscles: OXO, the company best known for its "Good Grips" kitchen products, is now moving into office supplies, medical devices, and baby products. The renowned Mayo Clinic partnered with Oxford University Press to publish a series of medical reference and textbooks. Michaels Stores, the craft specialty retailer, is testing an expansion into big cities rather than its traditional mid-sized markets. Zappos, the online shoe company, launched a print catalog called Zappos Life and is now sharing the lessons of its corporate culture with other companies. Home Depot is launching a Martha Stewart paint line. *Rolling Stone* is creating a restaurant. Stretching. Reaching. Questioning. Innovating. Surprising. These brands are making their customers down right curious about what's next!

A sneak peek

Like Leveen, I've been "noticing what I'm noticing" and one of the things I have been seeing is that more and more brands are opening up their "backrooms" to their customers. They are inviting them in to see the inner workings of the brand, from the people behind the brand to sharing employees' favorite products, to showcasing the way products are created and how other customers are using the items. They are responding to their customers' curiosity in novel ways.

This creative transparency taps wholly into a brand's heart and soul. Sharing this "insider" knowledge kindles customers' desires to be both "in the know" about brands they resonate with and gives them interesting stories to tell other like-minded friends and family members. Let's take a BrandAbout look at a few examples.

Boden, a UK clothing retailer, ran a series of photos entitled "The Story of a Boden Dress" on its website in 2009, showing customers just how a dress comes together for its brand. This series started with a frame of the ideas meeting and ran

through to the finalization of the outfit as pictured in the catalog and on the website. This peek into backstage or back office production may be something Boden merchants do day in and day out, but for customers, it's a chance to learn not only how a dress is made, but about the care and attention that Boden designers put into their patterns, their color choices, and their stitching details. It is a chance for Boden fashionistas both here and around the world to learn what makes this brand different.

J. Crew wants its shoppers to meet the woman behind all the design details, creative director, Jenna Lyons. Her monthly "Jenna's Picks" highlight her must-haves and might even rival Oprah's O list. Another internal designer, Jenny Cooper (mom of two) shares her favorite picks at Crewcuts. Customers love seeing these edited selections from style experts in the know. Additionally, for all the J. Crewaholics out there, the website gives its customers a sneak peek at one of its latest photo shoots.

Lands' End focused on two categories by creating interactive product websites to lure two different niche customer segments into two highly competitive product categories: swimsuits and backpacks. They called these sites "The Island" and "Pack-land," respectively, and encouraged customers to "play in their brand." On its main site, Lands' End features a social network for its mom audience entitled "What Moms Say," and includes product-specific testimonials about those very backpacks.

CHEFS is a destination site for those cooks looking for the best in kitchen products. One way it differentiates itself from other well-known companies competing in that space is to take advantage of its customers' competitive nature and offer meaningful contests. As an example, two merchandising-driven sweepstakes that customers could enter as I was working on this book were a Julia & Jacques Cooking at Home Sweepstakes (win a $1,000 CHEFS gift card) and an America's Test Kitchen Sweepstakes (win $5,000 worth of cookware plus $5,000 in cash). As a customer-centric merchant, I appreciate the extra level of attention the marketing professionals at CHEFS gave its contest entry forms. For the Julia (as in Child) and Jacques (as in Pepin) contest, in addition to just having the customers submit their name and email, it also asked a few brief but meaningful questions:

1. I tend to cook meals that are _____.
2. In my kitchen, I'll never be without _____.
3. When it comes to food, I most identify with _____.
4. My cooking idol/inspiration is _____.
5. When I'm in the kitchen, I become _____.

The answers to these savvy questions will be excellent conversation starters for its merchants to continue brainstorming innovative merchandising best practices.

L.L.Bean While J. Crew's tactic has been to feature just two of their lead designers, L.L.Bean chooses to have its customers meet more of its merchants and designers via its product videos. For example, customers can spend just over a minute of time with outerwear developers, A.J. Curran and Christine Wedge and succinctly learn why the Ascent Gore-Tex jacket may or may not be the one for them. Again, customers get a sense of real people behind the brand who share many of their same personal outdoor needs and concerns.

Orvis *The Dog Book* knows that dog lovers are a connected and passionate group, but it found out just *how much* when it received over 5,600 entries to its Cover Dog Contest. CEO Perk Perkins writes in the opening spread of the catalog, "We learned a lot from this experience. For one thing, we learned that our readers and customers are one extremely talented

bunch. We also learned that many of your dogs possess skills we never even knew existed. And, we learned that, at the end of the day, you really love your dogs. They represent family in the truest sense of the word, and your photos reflect that." This fall, *The Dog Book* catalog featured the winner front and center on the cover and nine other favorite entries on the inside spread. More contest photos were sprinkled throughout the catalog and you could watch the cover dog video online. No doubt about it, Orvis "gets" dog owners and it is apparent from this responsive outpouring, that customers resonate with the personal appeal of showing off their "family members."

PB Teen took the time in early 2009 to find out what was really important to its constantly evolving adolescent customers. One of its front covers depicted six teens with that exact question. Open the first inside spread and you'll see their answers: recycling, their family, their room, the environment, music, surfing. *PB Teen* then went on to position its products around those concerns—what I like to call purposeful merchandising. Know‑

ing teens value their space at home and consider their rooms a reflection of their personalities, a more recent catalog and web feature revolves around a "Design Your Own Bed" concept, even partnering with Benjamin Moore on wall colors. Very engaging, very personal.

Title Nine Missy Parks, founder of Title Nine, a women's athletic apparel brand, launched a website, "Time Out with Title Nine" as an online community for women on the move. Subjects range from "Missy's Musings," to "Working In Working

Out," to a "Focus On Product," which encompasses many of the sneak peek merchandising surprises previously mentioned such as behind-the-scenes photo shoots, in-house style-experts' picks, customer contests (surfboard), and more. Like the attention *PB Teen* pays to its target audience, Title Nine has always made it part of its brand to feature model athletes on its site and in its catalog. Parks' latest musing is personal and transparent and talks about learning curves. She invites answers from her customers to this curious question: "When's the last time you tried something for the first time?"

Curiosity is a trait that surrounds great brands inside and out and all around. Microsoft founder Bill Gates remarked, "If you give people tools, [and they use] their natural ability and their curiosity, they will develop things in ways that will surprise you very much beyond what you might have expected."

How will your brand exercise its curiosity muscle?

Be Insatiably Curious Homework

Bring out your inner Curious George and try a few of these ideas.

⫸ Just curious

Writer and poet Dorothy Parker said it most simply: "Try curiosity." In that indomitable spirit, why not try hosting your own brand Curiosity Day and see what happens. That's it. Don't over-plan or over-control it. Just see what you learn from your team members. Who knows? Maybe it will lead to your own version of a "Live in Color" or "Live Curious" philosophy!

))) Yoga for the brand

Professor Hal Gregersen said, "Studies have shown that creativity is close to 80 percent learned and acquired. We found that it's like exercising your muscles—if you engage in the actions, you build the skills." Why not engage in a stretching brandstorming session and wonder out loud about answers to this open-ended question: "What if our brand did _____?"

))) Behind the curtains

What goes on behind the scenes at your brand? Is it different than what goes on at your top three competitors? How can you show and tell relevant aspects of your story in ways that will engage your customers?

))) Stretching class

Fortune magazine reported that "to help prepare promising leaders for the future, companies are forcing their employees to take on new global risks." The article says that the greatest growth and opportunities are coming from outside the U.S. and that international assignments promote the greatest stretch. So whether your company is indeed global or made up of a party of one, you can think about stretch assignments. And, although you know you have my permission, you don't even need to leave your office! Poet Oliver Wendell Holmes said, "A person's mind stretched to a new idea never goes back to its original dimensions." Go forth and stretch!

Listen Actively

I HAVE A COLORFUL WORD on my desk as a reminder to do something that is not always top-of-mind for me. It simply says: LISTEN.

As fast-paced entrepreneurs running businesses, managing people, projects, schedules, and products, listening can sometimes fall off our to-do lists. We are rushed and busy people. We have decisions to make. Plans to execute. Visions to construct. Details to attend to. Places to be. Meetings to schedule. We don't have time to really pause and listen well. While we may see the value in making time, few of us actually do.

True listening takes an unbusy mindset and an unhurried presence. Listening takes concentration. Listening takes fortitude. Listening takes an open and careful spirit. Active listening is just plain hard work. We must schedule listening time on our daily calendar.

I am reminded of a typical fast-paced doctor's office visit. These days the patient needs to be ultra-prepared if she wants to make the most of her ten-minute maximum visit. Her questions are ready, her Internet information is in hand, and the pharmaceutical ad for the wonder-drug-with-all-the-side-effects is ripped out of the magazine. The doctor tries his best to diagnose the patient by asking all the right follow-up questions and skims her Internet printouts. As the patient answers with vague replies, prescriptions are written, tests are ordered, and the time together rapidly comes to end. As the doctor is on his way out the door, the patient more often than not will say, "By the way, doctor . . ." and proceed to tell the doctor what is truly bothering her. The doctor steps fully back into the room, sits down, and begins to listen to the real reason she has come to see him. The true conversation begins.

As brand builders, we don't want to be like rushed doctors. We need to be ready for these "by the way" conversations at the very start of our company-wide interactions with our customers and not hope that they happen by chance. We need to seek out these "by the way" listening opportunities with our employees, our customers, and our partners. As author Sue Patton Thoele reminds us, "Deep listening is miraculous for both listener and speaker. When someone receives us with open-hearted, non-judging, intensely interested listening, our spirits expand."

We need to be intensely interested brand listeners. Listening well can certainly help us expand our brand spirit. The insights and perspectives offered by our three significant resources—employees, customers, and partners—can lead to true breakthroughs. What percentage of your time do you spend listening to these important people? And just how do you do that?

Brands can practice active listening in a variety of different ways. Perhaps you already are listening in some of these ways to one of your key groups (for example, employees). If that method is providing fruitful results, why not try to incorporate that tool with other groups (customers or vendors) or try several different approaches across all three groups? I don't believe we can ever listen too much!

Face time from the top

Brand leaders must model this behavior for all their employees. In one of his first business books, Tom Peters encouraged leaders to practice "MBWA," that is, "management by wandering around." Those who stay hidden in their offices too busy to look up or out and engage in personal customer interaction are really missing out. They send a subliminal message that customer knowledge is good rhetoric and appropriate for "customer service people," but not an integrated brand practice.

Jorgen Vig Knudstorp, CEO of LEGO, the world's fourth largest toy company, regularly meets with adult fans of LEGO. In a *Harvard Business Review* conversation with Andrew O'Connell, he said, "An amazing number of grown-ups like to play with LEGOs. While we have 120 staff designers, we potentially have probably 120,000 volunteer designers we can access outside the company to help us invent. Perhaps most important, these super-users can articulate the product strengths and weaknesses that young children may sense but can't express." These interactions have become so important that LEGO has created two customer-driven programs: LEGO Ambassadors and a LEGO Certified Professionals program. These active customer listening programs not only keep the CEO in the loop but all members of the LEGO brand team.

Fortune magazine interviewed Best Buy's CEO Brian Dunn about how he stays connected to staff and customers. The magazine reported, "He posts questions to an employee website called Water Cooler, tracks customer sentiment on social media like Facebook and Twitter, attends focus groups, and invites customers to the company's leadership meetings." Dunn was quoted as saying, "One of my roles as CEO is to be the chief listener. I don't believe that the model is any longer that there are a few really smart people at the top of the pyramid that make all the strategic decisions. It is much more about being all around the enterprise and looking for people with great ideas and passionate points of view that are anchored to the business and connected to things our customers care about."

Papa John's founder John Schnatter went on a nationwide road trip to personally deliver pizzas to celebrate the company's 25th anniversary. He combined this with a hunt for his original 1972 Z28 Camaro that he sold in 1984 to finance his first Papa John's restaurant at the age of 22 (and yes, he found it!). After 25 years of running the world's third-largest pizza company, Schnatter still never tires of direct customer interaction. He prioritizes face time with his customers and has even incorporated the acronym of P.A.P.A. (People Are Priority Always) as part of the brand's core values.

As a brand leader, how much face time is built into your listening schedule?

Sounding boards

Do you ever wish you could just pick a few of your customers' brains? Maybe take them out for a long lunch and bounce a few ideas off them for their reactions? Or just sit back and let them tell you what's top of mind for them? If so, customer advisory boards are just the listening tool you need! Companies of all shapes and sizes are tapping into the wisdom of their customers through this listening method.

McDonald's launched a mom-driven Quality Correspondent program where moms from across the country go on McDonald's field trips to learn all about the company's inner workings and behind-the-scenes happenings. Recent trips have focused on the

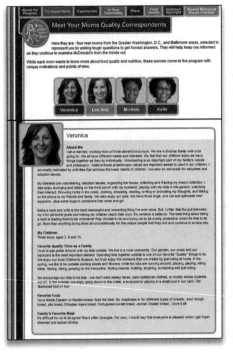

Happy Meal, from toy development to menu choices, and the making of McCafé, McDonald's new espresso-based coffee line. These moms then blog and post their findings to other customers via the *mcdonaldsmom.com* website. This transparent mom-to-mom sounding board allows McDonald's to see first-hand how its brand is being perceived and what is top of mind for moms in making fast food choices for their families.

Online clearance outlet, Overstock.com, took a broader approach with its sounding board, opening it up to a 300-plus active member group. Calling it the Private Lounge, Overstock.com reported in *Retail Touchpoints,* "in its first year, the community has helped revitalize their Club O loyalty program, refine its popular television advertising, reinstate some of its customers' most-missed web features and reinvigorate their holiday shopping sales." By regularly and actively listening to a broad cross-section of its customers, Overstock.com not only stays in touch with its customers' changing needs but relies on this sounding board to help tweak its promotional strategies.

Duluth Trading, a company specializing in workwear and gear for those in trades, relies heavily on its customer panels. These working-guy-and-gal groups keep Duluth Trading Co. closely in touch with the real on-

the-job challenges of these professionals and no doubt are the
reasons behind many of their
product innovations.

One of my clients, Christian
Brothers Services, just implemented this idea in order to get
a better understanding of its customers' changing needs as pend-
ing healthcare reform threatens
to change the entire way benefits are delivered. The new board
of advisors each felt honored to be asked to participate and have
already shared valuable insights with the CBS managers.

How can you create a sounding board either formally or informally?

Simply hang out and observe

Leadership experts James Kouzes and Barry Posner remind us
that "the best leaders are able to bring their people into the future
because they engage in the oldest form of research: They observe
the human condition." Indeed, an important part of listening is
conscientious watching, focusing on what's not being said, and
reading between the lines.

Mickey Drexler, J. Crew's CEO, attributes some of the brand's
success to both his power of observation and his ability to teach
the store associates how to do the same. He regularly walks into
his stores and pays close attention to what competitive shopping
bags his customers are carrying. He likes to listen in on conversations his customers are having as they browse. And he simply
point blank asks them, "Anything we can do better?"

Like Drexler, I did some creative eavesdropping when I was
working for a client that marketed to teens. Knowing how fickle

that audience is, I did my best to immerse myself in their favorite websites, magazines, restaurants, and teen stores like American Eagle and Abercrombie. I "hung out" in the bustling teen department at Nordstrom on several occasions and even went in the dressing rooms with my own set of clothes to try on, so I could overhear girls' comments about the clothes they were trying on and the words they used to describe those experiences. It was enlightening to listen in to their worlds and their concerns.

It might be hard to talk women who have the resources and inclination to buy and ride their own motorcycles into going to a Tupperware party, but just invite them to a Harley Garage Party event. They'll be there in droves. In some ways, you could say it's a modern twist on the old-fashioned practice of quilting bees. There's really only one rule at these meetings: no men. The parties are intentionally set up as "intimidation free zones" where women can investigate the sport before deciding to get involved and can circulate among female riders of all experience levels. Garage parties teach women the differences between the various makes and models of Harleys, the necessities of proper gear and clothing, and how to customize a motorcycle to a rid-

er's personal preference. They also educate women on another very important topic: how to lift a Harley without breaking a nail! These nationwide motorcycle open houses keep Harley professionals in the important "pre-customer thought process" loop in a first-hand way. No doubt, this personal level of engagement has helped fuel the record-setting, double digit upward trend of women riders.

How have you made time to hang out with your customers lately?

Encourage pain-point confessions

Too many companies lack courage. I'm not talking about Big Courage (like taking risks to launch new innovative products or explore new untapped markets), but the everyday kind of courage to do the hard but necessary things to keep a brand relevant and purposeful to its customers. Like the lion in the *Wizard of Oz,* many brands simply lack the everyday courage to connect with their customers. I think they are afraid of what they might learn.

It takes courage to hear things about your customers' brand experiences that are less than ideal. But making time to find out just what is bothering your customers can lead to brand breakthroughs. Having the courage to simply ask, "What do you find difficult in doing business with us?" or "What stops you from buying our product?" or "Where else do you shop for products like ours?" or even "Where are we making it too complicated for you?" can yield great insights into your customers' pain points. Courageous companies encourage pain-point confessions.

Two brave and bold men who have done more than any others to change the way business is done today also believe in the value of paying attention to your customers' pain points. Microsoft chairman, Bill Gates notes, "Your most unhappy customers are your greatest source of learning." Amazon founder Jeff Bezos speaks to the downside of *not* listening to your customers' pain points, "If you make a customer unhappy in the physical world, they might each tell six friends. If you make customers unhappy on the Internet, they can each tell 6,000 friends."

Target, one of America's most admired companies, published an invitation in the *Denver Post* at the beginning of the summer. It simply said, "Tell us what *more* we can do for you." At the end of the summer it ran a bright red, two-page spread with the headline "You asked for more. Here goes." The ad outlined five specific things customers wanted and exactly how Target is responding. Plain and simple. Target was courageous and asked. Customers answered. Target listened. Target took action.

Charles Schwab, a leading investment brokerage, takes the art of customer listening seriously. It wanted to be sure that potential customers knew that it was different than its stuffy financial counterparts. "Charles Schwab" became the accessible "Chuck" and a "Talk to Chuck" multimedia advertising campaign was born. This long-running and successful marketing effort is built around a series of customer thought bubbles that encourages people to "Start talking. We're listening." Each thought bubble is a conversational snippet that reveals thoughts and patterns going on inside a prospective customer's mind. The intimate and accurate nature of the thought bubbles ("I don't want to work forever," or "I've lost too much to be paying this much") clearly shows that the team at Charles Schwab has listened well to its customers' pain points and is prepared to meet its customers' changing financial needs.

Chase, the consumer banking brand of JPMorgan Chase & Co., also launched a campaign around its customers' pain points. Entitled "Chase What Matters," these messages remind customers that Chase knows exactly what to do when your card gets stolen or when you are worried about overdrafts or when you need a simple and convenient way to check your balances. Chase wants its customers to know that it keeps tabs on their pain points and is ready to respond.

Sometimes pain can be a hard thing to articulate just right. (MasterCard has an ad that says, "What if it's broke and you don't know it?") Customers also like to be positive. Brand leaders need to find ways to probe for customers' discontent if their customers are not immediately forthcoming. Peter Drucker, the father of modern management, reminds us that "The most important thing in communication is to hear what isn't being said."

How will you go about drawing out your customers' pain points?

Group genius

Listening to one customer at a time certainly has its benefits. So does listening to many at once. I like psychologist Keith Sawyer's term for this: "group genius." In a book by that same title, Sawyer writes about the art of collaborating creatively with customers. Pulling customers together formally or informally can lead to both small and big sparks.

I have conducted customer listening sessions with companies in industries ranging from country clubs to social expression to women's and children's apparel to inspirational gifts. They are very simple meetings. While we have an agenda, we are always prepared to go where the customers lead. One of the benefits of these roundtables is that we can see our customers up close, that is, what clothes they wear, how they carry themselves, hear how they express (or not) certain brand feelings. These are things that cannot be done by phone or email. Just "being with" the customers is constructive time well spent in truly "walking a mile in their shoes."

One of my clients, Orient Expressed, an upscale children's clothing company, did just this. The two founders, Bee Fitzpatrick and Dabney Jacob, wanted to really get inside the minds of their busy mom customers—and have fun doing it! They knew their marketplace was changing and they needed first hand information from their best customers. So they gathered a group of "Orient Expressed moms" together, started the sharing time with an evening cocktail party at Jacob's home and then brought the group to the company's New Orleans office for a day where we continued

spending time in playful conversation about their product line. Fitzpatrick and Jacob felt the time together was "amazing" and "very valuable" and "clarifying." The customers enjoyed the like-minded camaraderie, sharing pictures of their children in clothing from Orient Expressed and by the time the

day was over they had befriended one another! This photo was taken at the end of the day of playfully, but strategically, "walking a mile in their sandals."

In addition to being insightful for all the brand team members and full of actionable nuances, these sessions all had one thing in common: customers are eager to bond with other like-minded souls. They are all passionate about their favorite products and in true party format, try to "sell" the others around the table. Their enthusiasm is fun to observe. These get-togethers remind me of what happens when my nonstop, talkative Italian family meets for holiday celebrations, complete with waving hands and high emotions. The energy is high and you never know what you might learn!

Some companies have institutionalized listening into more for-

malized and proactive websites that
are open to all who want to participate, a form of "crowdsourcing" if you
will. Dell has its IdeaStorm™ community; P&G has Connect + Develop;
IBM has MyDeveloperWorks.com;
Best Buy has BestBuyIdeaX.

Dell is listening. Dell's IdeaStorm™ community, powered by Salesforce Ideas, was the inspiration that led the way to Dell's new ProSupport services. Salesforce.com helps companies learn from their customers every day. **www.salesforce.com**

In addition to tapping into its customers' group genius, Best Buy was
one of the first companies to take its
traditional employee suggestion box
and formalize it into a social networking internal community called Blue
Shirt Nation. Since then, Blue Shirt Nation has transitioned their
internal "group genius" into BSNMix, an even more usable format
for employees and Best Buy leaders. I like what their site says ever
so simply and directly: "Stay connected. Share stuff. Collaborate.
Mix connects us and makes us more valuable to each other and
our customers." Isn't that the real purpose of active listening—to
become a more valuable brand to your customers?

But it isn't just tech companies or packaged goods companies
that are tapping into their customers' collective wisdom. America's
most ubiquitous coffee shop, Starbucks, created MyStarbucksIdea.
com, where it entices customers to participate in this way: "What
would make your Starbucks experience perfect? We know you've
got ideas—big ideas, little ideas, maybe even totally revolutionary
ideas—and we want to hear them all. That's why we created My
Starbucks Idea. So you can share the ideas that matter to you and
you can find out how we're putting those ideas to work. Together,
we will shape the future of Starbucks." How many companies
aspire to want their customer experiences to be perfect?

These crowdsourcing sites tap into the collective wisdom of
user experience and give companies real time feedback on a

variety of product, promotional, and internal brand challenges. Whether this "group genius" effort is undertaken formally or informally, brands that practice active listening in this way multiply their learnings quickly.

Have you fully leveraged the potential of your group genius?

Homework for your customers

Can you remember back to grade school? Usually your most demanding teachers accelerated your learning process by having you *do* something in relation to a lesson: make dioramas, put on a drama, dress up in a period costume, create a recipe from the country you were studying, and so forth. Brands that vigorously listen to their customers often invite them to engage in "doing" activities as well.

One of my clients, CHEFS, regularly taps its customers for insights. Tim Littleton, CHEFS' president and CEO, says, "Branding cannot be determined only by the creative and marketing teams who are paid for such things. Customers get to vote, and it is their perception of your brand that is most meaningful. At CHEFS we continuously survey our customers online during their shopping experience and regularly post-purchase. Spending adequate time reviewing and analyzing customer purchase data will help reveal who you are as a brand. At CHEFS we find this process invaluable and will typically find more useful nuggets of information each time we go through this process. Based on this data we often adjust our strategy, which may go against conventional wisdom of the industry "experts," but in the end provides a better experience for our customers and ultimately more profitable results for CHEFS."

Thomas Nelson, a Christian book publisher, invites customers to become book review bloggers. In exchange for crafting 200 word reviews on any consumer retail website, readers get free books. This feedback loop keeps Thomas Nelson's authors in tune with their readers and corporately builds goodwill. This publisher knows that readers are often closet writers and is tapping into this avocation brilliantly.

Ben&Jerry's, the social mission-minded ice cream company based in Vermont, encourages its customers to become "Chunk Spelunkers." True to its brand, Ben&Jerry's way of involving customers is quirky and light-hearted. These spelunkers ("ones who mine through pints of Ben&Jerry's for the big chunks!") are the first to be in-the-know about new flavors and may be invited to become Honorary Flavor Judicators or Flavor Cultivators. Its website provides a forum for comments or complaints (they want their customers' experiences to be "pure euphoria") and asks customers to either suggest a new flavor or recommend the resurrection of an old flavor. Ben&Jerry's knows that its customers have the gift of gab and it wants to leverage that!

What homework can you ask your customers to do?

Author Brenda Ueland (of "moodling" fame) understands both the generative and regenerative power of listening. She writes, "Listening is a magnetic and strange thing, a creative force. When we really listen to people there is an alternating current, and this recharges us so that we never get tired of each other. We are constantly being re created."

Sometimes, unintentionally, brands act as though they are tired of their customers. So, in the spirit of brand re-creation and of becoming a more valuable brand to your customers, why not try a few of these exercises?

Listen Actively Homework

))) Thought bubbles

Draw ten empty thought bubbles. Pause. Think about ten things that your customers might be thinking about as they make decisions regarding your brand. Write those in the thought bubbles. Then, go find ten customers and give them ten empty thought bubbles on different colored paper and ask them the same question. Post your answers all around your meeting room. See how your answers compare. How close were you to capturing your customers' feelings? Take it a step further and create a Charles Schwab inspired "Talk to Chuck" campaign for your brand.

))) The heart of the matter

After each sale or transaction, have your salespeople ask your customers, "By the way, is there anything *more* that we can do for you?" (Place a "By the way" feedback button at the end of each online transaction as well.) Track these responses for a month and have a "By the way" conversation about these learnings with the leadership team. What will you do about what you've discovered?

))) Purposeful eavesdropping

Divide your team up into pairs and have them go out two by two to simply hang out in different locations where your customers are gathered. Be as inconspicuous as possible. Pretend you are a reporter (like Nike's field reporters!) and observe carefully. Take detailed notes of everything you see and hear, what they are wearing (shoes, handbags or messenger bags, jewelry), to what state of mind they appear to be in (relaxed, hurried), to whom they seem to be with (kids, girlfriends, co-workers, alone), and to what kind of conversations they are having. Note the kind of technology they are or are not using (smart phones/laptops/MP3 players/e-readers) and any other specifics you deem noteworthy in relation to your brand experience. Have each twosome paint a word picture of five to ten customers. Come back as a team and share your notes. What are the common denominators among everything you have observed and heard from the customers? Make a collage of these "What makes our customers tick . . . " insights and share it throughout the company.

Conduct Tête-á-Têtes

I'll never forget the first time I saw our friends Don and Millie work across from one another at their antique double-sided desk. My husband and I met them when they were in their late sixties. By that point they had been married over 40 years and were quite used to doing most everything as a team, whether it was running their business consultancy, their thousand-acre ranch, or their numerous volunteer and church activities. It all happened around that one desk. It was their action hub. She was on one side. He was on the other. They heard each other's phone conversations; they interrupted each other's thought processes; they checked in with each other in real time. They shared a brain.

I've often thought that most businesses would benefit greatly from double-sided desks with a member from the company on one side and an actual customer on the other. This would take the "walk a mile in your customers' shoes" concept to the next level. Instead of Tweeting or Facebooking or surveying or focus grouping or even worse, simply guessing, the brand team members would have ready access to their customers' thoughts and desires. The brand team member could ask customers functional questions like "Would you pay $39.95 for this widget?" or "How have we made this design too complicated?" or "Would your child really wear this striped and polka dot combo?" to more emotional driven queries like "How have we let you down?" or "What do you like better about our competitors' shopping experience?" or, simply, a no-agenda "What's on your mind?" probe.

Customers could come in for hour meetings and spend time in various departments having meaningful across-the-desk conversations. It could become the best business practice ever. Employees could look customers in the eye. Customers could look employees in the eye. They could listen to one another. A lot could happen. A lot could change for brands. These business tête-à-têtes could be very powerful. Unfortunately, I've yet to see a double-sided desk in the workplace.

What seems to be more prevalent in the business world are large, can't-see-over-the-top, often quite intimidating, silos. Yes, silos like the tall, cylindrical ones you see in farm country that hold grain and hay. It's one of the most talked about subjects in

my business consultancy. Company executives either tell me they don't want be siloed or that they don't believe they are. Both are troublesome dilemmas. The ones that say they don't want to be siloed often have a great desire to act as one company but don't want to do the work it takes to actually de-silo. The ones that think they don't have silos are often mistaken.

Silos exist in all sizes of companies. Silos can be as prevalent in two-person partnerships, family-run businesses, and Fortune 100- to Fortune 1000-sized companies. From both employee and customer points of view, silos are the antithesis of double-sided desks. Silos sap brand energy and turn the focus away from the customer and the competition to the company itself, often building self-serving fiefdoms and using brand-building potential on internal turf battles. Silos exhaust me.

My hat goes off to Patagonia, the environmentally responsible outdoor clothing company founded by Yvon Chouinard. Patagonia just doesn't "do silos." When I spoke with Kevin Churchill, Director of Merchandising, he shared the practical example of all their channels sharing one warehouse. "Patagonia believes in a one brand, one message, one customer philosophy. We all support the company in total. We want our customers to get our product wherever it suits them best—whatever channel is most convenient for them. If our warehouse is out, we're happy to send them to one of our wholesale partners like REI or Moosejaw. We don't compete against ourselves. We're all on the same page. We just don't do silos." This global company lives and breathes a non-silo culture. There are no divisions at Patagonia.

Life's a beachball

Susan Scott, author of *Fierce Conversations: Achieving Success at Work and in Life One Conversation at a Time* writes brilliantly and helpfully on the topic of silos. She uses the analogy of a beachball to make her point. Scott says that people in the various divisions of a company naturally work all day every day in their particular colored stripe (accounting, marketing, customer service, operations, or merchandising) and therefore see all corporate decisions through that particular color or lens. They see a red perspective all day or a green or a blue or a yellow one. We need each of those perspectives but we need a more comprehensive, outer-directed view as well. Customers look at a company and its actions holistically; they see the entire beachball. Think about your own experience. If you try to order an item online and it's out of stock, you don't necessarily fault the forecasting or inventory department, you simply get frustrated with the company overall. The more companies can operate as a beachball culture, collaborating, talking across desks with one another, seeing things from multiple perspectives, putting the needs of the customers first versus their own departments', the better.

Scott firmly believes that the conversations people have truly *are* the relationships. She is an advocate for real dialogue and honest tête-à-têtes. "The simplest definition of a fierce conversation is one in which we come out from behind ourselves, into the conversation, and make it real. While most people are uncomfortable with real, it is the unreal conversations that should scare us to death. Why? Because they are incredibly expensive, for organizations and for individuals. Most organizations want to feel they are having a real conversation with their employees, their customers, and their evolving marketplaces. And most individuals want to feel they are having conversations that build their world of meaning." She is anti-image management, false corporate nods (where you seemingly agree but have no intention of following that particular course of action), and hiding behind the status quo. I introduce her work to all my clients and I give them a large inflatable beachball as a visible reminder.

Companies accomplish de-siloed beachball-esque behavior in several ways. One of my clients actually gave out small sqeezeable beach "stress" balls emblazoned with its company logo to all its employees. The idea it wanted to reinforce was that most times internal job stress is happening because employees are not acting like a beachball—they are getting bogged down in turf battles or silo miscommunications.

Proctor and Gamble has "huddle rooms" to encourage collaboration. Other companies have blogs or their versions of fireside chats. The Ritz-Carlton has a tradition called the "lineup" which president and COO Simon Cooper explained in *Forbes*: "The concept comes from the early restaurants of France, where the chef got the whole team and all the waiters and waitresses and the maître d' together at 5:30 in the evening. It's a sort of round table. Everybody is there. The chef communicates what they are going to be serving. For the Ritz-Carlton, we want every single hotel, everywhere in the world, every partner, every shift to utilize lineup which typically takes around 15 minutes every day. Part of the lineup everywhere around the world is a "wow story," which means talking about great things that our ladies and gentlemen have done. That is a wonderful training and communication tool, where every department layers on the department message. And, it's based on having the same message everywhere, everyday and then each hotel layers on its own message."

How well and how often do you listen to people in different stripes? I believe that there is a direct correlation between how well company employees listen to one another and how well they listen to their customers. Companies that have developed good listening skills internally usually take those same skills with them externally in connecting with their customers. Michael Dell has long been an advocate of customer listening: "These conversations are going to occur whether you like it or not. . . . do you want to be part of that? My argument is that you absolutely do. You can learn from that. You can improve your reaction time. And you can be a better company by listening and being involved in that conversation." Mark Jarvis, Dell's chief marketing officer believes that "listening to our customers is the most perfect form of marketing you can have."

In an interview with *Harvard Business Review*, Dick Harrington, former CEO of Thomson Reuters, said emphatically that "it always comes back to the customers and you have to *maniacally* know your customers and drive everything from that." While many business leaders will give the corporate nod to this, not everyone actually puts this into practice. "The biggest reason people don't do this," Harrington says, "and we've seen it a lot, is that they think working in an industry a long time means they know everything about the customers' needs."

Question everything

"Question everything." This is the advice from German scientist Georg Christoph Lichtenberg. As an outsider-insider to my clients, my role is often "Questioner-in-Chief" (to use a term borrowed from Tom Peters). Recently, I was leading a brandstorming session with one of my financial services clients when one of the employees pulled me aside during a break and said, "I didn't want to ask this question in front of the group because I was afraid it would seem silly . . ." and then proceeded to ask me a very important and profound question pertinent to our strategic planning work. I encouraged her to ask that question when we regrouped because I wanted her to experience the collective "aha!" that would arise from her provocative question.

Since then, I've been pondering the importance of questions and the cultural dynamics that enable some companies to encourage a healthy questioning behavior while other companies seem to squash it without saying a word. Questioning is so often the precursor to innovation. Alfred North Whitehead, a British mathematician and philosopher, said, "The 'silly question' is the first intimation of some totally new development." After more than two decades of questioning, I have come to believe that there really are *no* silly questions.

Early in his career, Clayton Christensen, Harvard professor and business expert, learned the importance of asking the right questions. In a community service talk he said, "Most of the world operates as if we believe that the critical skill society needs of us is to know the right answers. Too often, as a result, we overlook an obvious fact: finding the right answer is impossible unless we have asked the right question. Unfortunately, most of us are so eager to formulate the right answer and then begin implementing it that we often forget to think about whether the right question has been asked."

A questioning mindset is a humble mindset. It says, "I don't have all the answers. I am willing to learn new information. I am willing to be wrong. I am willing to change my assumptions." What questions is your brand grappling with or perhaps *should* be grappling with these days? Taking time to think through the questions that are of utmost importance to your customers and to your company will help provide a strategic framework for all your brand's activities.

Even Jerry Greenfield's (of Ben & Jerry's fame) lighthearted question, "If it's not fun, why do it?" is one of crucial importance to its brand. Fun is an attribute at the top of Ben & Jerry's brand and product fit charts. It is even a tab on its website. Having worked with this brand, I know first-hand that fun is taken seriously and that this question is one that frames its decision-making.

In 2003, Frederick F. Reichheld wrote an article for the *Harvard Business Review* called "The One Number You Need to Grow." His research showed that if brands concentrated on improving just one measure, it should be the answer to this question asked of their customers: "How likely is it that you would recommend our company to a friend or colleague?" Since that time, a whole business based on this simple question has been launched (Net Promoter) and several books (*Ultimate Question*) have been published. Yes, this is indeed an important question.

Social activist Fran Peavey says, "A very powerful question may not have an answer at the moment it is asked. It will sit rattling in the mind for days or weeks as the person works on an answer.

If the seed is planted, the answer will grow. Questions are alive." So, in that spirit, here are a few questions to ponder.

First and foremost, do you cultivate a question-asking environment?

Without the freedom to raise questions or question decisions appropriately, your brand may have a blind spot. At Chinaberry, a multi-channeler of children's books and other treasures for the whole family, Ann Ruethling, vice president and founder, has created an environment "that any question that is asked gets an open and honest answer. Once enough employees realize that no question is going to be laughed at or ignored or cause problems, they feel comfortable questioning. We enjoy provocative questions and, when working on a project, we include those employees directly involved in the project at hand, as well as those employees sort of superficially involved because often they are the ones to offer a fresh viewpoint."

Bill Boonstra, owner of Bluestone Perennials, for 30 years a family-owned and operated gardening business, asks, "Would you want your daughter/son to work for Bluestone?" It's a good reflective question on the nature of your present work environment. Is it a collaborative place where employees are energized by what they do? Are people smiling?

Second, can you handle the answers to tough questions?

Many brands have solid customer loyalty programs in place. These are indeed important parts of retention strategies. But take a moment to turn that question around for your brand. Just how loyal is your brand to your customers? What have you done for *them* lately?

Part of what's made Chinaberry successful for 27 years is this extreme level of customer care. It isn't just a friendly customer service experience; it goes deeper than that. Ruethling says, "So much of what we do here is intuitive. And it comes from a personal place. For example, unless one of us can personally picture wearing this item or having it in her home on a permanent basis, we wouldn't *think* of trying to sell it to anyone. It would just seem wrong to us. People already have enough stuff they don't need without us trying to sell them something they won't use or like. We see too many brands selling more than enough of that kind of product and it makes us wince. We always ask, 'Will this item truly enrich the life of the person we hope will buy it?'"

Boonstra agrees wholeheartedly. One of his company's main questions is: "Are we doing what's best for our customers—not necessarily what's best or easiest for us?" He adds that he also likes to ask, "How would you handle that order or contact if you knew it was your mother-in-law (assuming you love your mother-in-law!)"?

Madeleine Mellini is the vice president of communications for TouchMath, a multi-sensory teaching and learning math program. She wants to know from her customers how they measure the effectiveness of TouchMath. Answers to this question not only help its product development and marketing teams, but also provide insights into Reinhold's question of the likelihood that TouchMath customers would recommend these products to other teachers and parents.

Gina Valentino, president of Hemisphere Marketing, a consultancy specializing in creative marketing and database solutions, told me: "Often I talk about the health of the customer file. When customer buying activity decreases, it means you're not listening. Customers are constantly telling you what they like about your company—look at the data. When you are truly attentive to your customers, you are supporting the relationship with the products and services you offer because you've listened. You listen—and respond with new merchandise, new services, new marketing and new creative."

So take some time to question your culture, your customers and your results. And then ask Dr. Phil's favorite question: "How is this working for you?"

Beyond the name tag

In a *HarvardBusiness.org* blog entitled, "The Real Secret of Thoroughly Excellent Companies," Peter Bregman interviews Michael Newcombe, the general manager of the Four Seasons, and discovers that he practices what he calls "proximity management." "Every month he meets informally with each employee group. No agenda. No speeches. Just conversation. He walks the property regularly. He asks employees about their families, brings donuts, arranges for birthday parties and softball tournaments. He gets beyond the name tag."

I am an advocate of both of Newcombe's practices—proximity management and being the Questioner-in-Chief. As a brand leader, how can you *not* stay close to both your employees and your customers? How else do you gain insights, continue learning, and keep the brand relevant? Arie de Gues, an expert in organizational learning, reminds leaders, "Your ability to learn faster than your competition is your only sustainable competitive advantage." Is your brand in a learning mode? And, even more importantly, in a "learning-faster-than-the-competitors" mode?

Some companies do appoint a Chief Learning Officer or a Customer Insights Officer or even a Chief Customer Officer. I like the "C" aspect of these roles as it signifies their importance to the organization. I also like having a seasoned professional to synthesize all the findings. But what I like even more is making these activities part of everyone's job. Shouldn't everyone involved in the brand engage customers, gather useful grassroots information for product development, market creation, competitive tracking, and improve the customer experience? Shouldn't these weekly findings be the heart of the staff meetings, the huddles, and the employee blogs? Wouldn't these types of conversations insure a true customer-centric beachball culture?

Debi Pelican, Supervisor, Customer and Industry Research for Colorado Springs Utilities, couldn't agree more. Her team takes listening a step further: "In order to supremely understand our customers, we must immerse ourselves in their space. And, that may mean going to Chuck E. Cheese pizza when you yourself have no kids but are marketing to those moms, or ducking into a Cabela's if you market to a group of outdoor-oriented men. We must find ways to be 'one with them.' Listen, watch, share stories. Only when we feel our customers' culture viscerally can we bring them what they want."

Frank Blake, CEO of Home Depot, also likes wandering around unannounced in the company's 1,900 U.S. stores. *The Financial Times* interviewed him about finding out what's on the mind of the frontline workers: "You need to create an environment where people feel free to say what they think. And that's easier said than done. I need to keep in mind that people are going to be saying that everything is great even when there are problems. An email suggestion box gives an interesting insight into where people's frustrations are, what's bothering them. Otherwise, everything will be fine—until it is falling around your head." I firmly believe that if you get behind the name tag, you'll often also get behind "everything's fine" too!

Getting beyond the name tag (whether with your employees or your generic customer demographic data) means that companies are always in school—learning, growing, changing, and evolving. When Coach, a leading American marketer of fine accessories and gifts, recently launched a new collection of handbags and accessories called Poppy, it ran a contest asking women aged 16 to 28 to create an online scrapbook page describing their own "Poppy Girl" personality. With a direct and fun call to "Let their inner Poppy shine!" Coach received thousands of entries. This scrapbook artwork gave the company much more insight than simply knowing that it was targeting women in this age group. The adjectives, drawings, and pictures they used gave the company deep insight into its customers' personalities.

E.&J. Gallo Winery launched an ad campaign that tells its customers it "gets" them. In the "How Do You Breathe?" print series for its Turning Leaf wine, Gallo makes the connection between wine and women needing a chance to breathe. One of the ads features a casually dressed female from Parker, Colorado with this handwritten quote: "I am not the sum of my responsibilities. I am not a soccer mom, or a statistic, or anything else other people think I am. I am real. I am true. I am alive and right now I am taking a minute to remember that and to breathe." What woman in America doesn't need a reminder to breathe? That Gallo gets this and connects its brand to a top-of-mind need for its customers shows that it, too, goes beyond the simple demographics of its business.

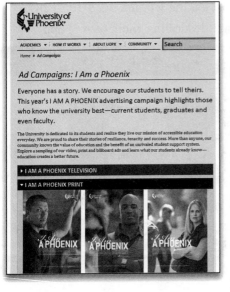

The University of Phoenix also went "beyond the name tag" when it featured student stories in a print and TV campaign called "I Am Phoenix." These profiles of real students, graduates and faculty helped to put a real "face" on the brand for those considering this campus and online degree program.

The Zagatization process

I'm quite sure that Nina and Tim Zagat had no idea that the process they casually started in 1979 around the dinner table with their friends would turn into both such a success for them and the beginning of businesses harnessing customers' opinions in a big way. According to its website, Zagat believes that the "shared opinions of thousands of avid consumers with real experiences are inherently more accurate than the opinions of just one or two critics."

When is the last time you made a purchase without checking to see what other customers had to say? I call it the Zagatization process and most consumers now feel that it's irresponsible not to! Trip Advisor does it. Amazon does it. Zappos does it. Harley does it. Orvis does it. Best Buy does it. FreshDirect does it. James Avery does it. It's become a business norm. A *BusinessWeek* story headlined, "How Amazon is Turning Opinions into Gold" elaborated: "Customer reviews are as common as hyperlinks and a retail website that does not have feedback loops is considered passé or irrelevant. In fact, more than 5 million consumers have posted tens of millions of reviews on Amazon." Amazon even has a "Senior Manager of Community." This position belongs to Russell Dicker, and in that same article he states, "What we try to spend our time on is harnessing customer passion."

Brands harness customer passion in a plethora of ways. Fresh-Direct Inc. is an online grocery delivery service in New York and its chairman and CEO Rick Braddock believes in "managing with intense customer focus." He's a big believer and practitioner of customer surveys. In a *Wall Street Journal* article, he explained that his company runs surveys weekly, and that those surveys are at the center of its understanding of customers. While some companies use customer feedback for business decisions, others use it right in the business processes. James Avery, a family-owned jewelry retailer, counts heavily on its customers' comments and stories and puts those words to work for the brand. In an interview at *eMarketingandCommerce.com*, John McCullough, director of marketing for James Avery, explains, "We don't use conventional selling copy online or in our catalogs—it's not the voice of our brand. However, we were comfortable using our customers' comments and stories. We believed content coming from them would resonate more with our customers. We let their content become the copy for our product."

Constant cocktail party

I like to encourage companies to think of the conversations they are having with their customers like the hum of a constant cocktail party. At the best of these gatherings, you get to flit around and mingle and make small talk that days later might lead to big talk. This cocktail party chatter can happen in person at events or online. Rick Lepley, CEO of A.C. Moore, a leading retailer of arts and crafts supplies, is quoted in *STORES* magazine as saying his customers are a "very, very talkative group. They love to express themselves any way they can and share their ideas with each other. Really, it's amazing how much they are online talking."

Leslie Prevish, Harley-Davidson's Women's Outreach Manager, spends her work life creating opportunities for this intentional chatter to occur. In addition to Harley Garage Parties, Harley sponsors major events like the AMA International Women and Motorcycling Conference. The theme of the latest conference was "Riding to New Heights" and gathered over 1000 female riders for four days of riding, learning, and networking, and no doubt, lots of cocktail party-like exchanges!

GE created its own global cocktail party. Here's an excerpt from how the company described its Global Customer Summit on one of its websites:

"Customers in traditional ethnic dress. The murmur of translations and whispers in foreign languages. Asian potato cakes, rice cracker snacks and green tea. The excitement of customers anxious to learn from GE's top leaders. This was the experience of GE's Global Customer Summit. . . . Approximately 160 customers and regional leaders from Africa, Taiwan, India, Southeast Asia, Kazakhstan, Korea, and Japan came together for a week of learning and networking. Previous meetings were smaller and region-specific. This year the Summit brought seven regions together to create a larger, more encompassing global perspective. Customers were thrilled about the chance to mix with other regions, as it facilitated broader learning. What most impressed the global customers was the extensive amount of interaction they had with GE's top leaders. The participation of GE's top leaders showed commitment to the company's global strategy. The leaders were open, honest and developed relationships with many of the customers."

Conduct Tête-á-Têtes Homework

It's always a good time to practice better internal and external listening. Try these ideas:

⫸ The name game

The U.S. Postal Service ran a campaign last year that featured a twist on the "Hello, My Name Is . . ." name tags. These tags enabled co-workers to share little tidbits about themselves in non-threatening and humorous ways such as, "My office nickname is . . ." or "My favorite way to look busy is . . ." or "My favorite website is . . ." or "My dream job is . . ." This campaign cut through the direct mail clutter that usually accumulates in my mailbox. It made me stop and think about how little we often know about co-workers within our own departments, let alone those outside. At a recent strategic planning session with a client whose employees all worked together for over 10 years, I asked: "What job in the company, other than the one you have now, would you be most interested in and why?" Their answers were delightfully surprising to all!

Why not brainstorm a few fun phrases like these (for example: "My favorite thing to do outside of work is . . ." or "The best part of my job is . . .") and incorporate them into your next company-wide meeting? Perhaps you'll learn something new about the people working not just in your beachball stripe, but in the stripes around you!

⫸ Question marks

Dick Harrington, former CEO of Thomson Reuters, the world's leading source of information for businesses and professionals advises, "Find your ten smartest customers and talk to them; those are the ones who can actually give you valuable information. It's about spending time with them and going over 10 to 15 questions to learn about how they use the product and what you can do to make their lives easier. From those questions, you'll probably get another 15 to 20. That's a great start and you can use that information to consider other more structured methodologies for more specific feedback." So, gather an interdepartmental team together and have each person write down 10 questions he or she would like to ask your customers. Compile all the lists and post them for the team to see. Then, working with a beachball mindset, cull the list to the ten most vital questions for the brand and propose them to your customers, in person, by phone, or by email. Circle back as a team and review those answers.

ᗰ To Zagat or not to Zagat?

There's really only one answer to that question in today's marketing environment—product reviews by customers (both good and bad) are a must! *Retail Customer Experience* reported a Nielsen study that found 70 percent of shoppers say they trust consumer opinions posted on retail websites. Conduct a BrandAbout review of ten sites outside your industry and see what product review practices you can borrow! If your brand is not yet offering product reviews, brandstorm how to get started, and fast! If you are already practicing this, how can you make it even easier for customers to share their feedback? How can you leverage the information they are sharing in a more beachball way?

5

Dare Yourself and Your Brand

REMEMBER the truth or dare games you played in grade school? "I dare you to leave a note in Eddie's locker!" or "I dare you to call Bobby's house!" Or the ultimate dare (which eventually led to the next game of, well, you remember, spin the bottle): "I dare you to kiss Bruce!" Those dares felt quite adventurous back then and not very achievable. But even if we tried and failed, we always stood a bit taller, felt a bit bolder, and acted a bit braver after our efforts. It seems as though we take fewer chances as we get older. As adults, when was the last time you dared yourself to do something meaningful? As brand leaders, when is the last time you dared your brand to do something outrageous? Is it time?

Years ago, *Good to Great* author Jim Collins dared companies to set BHAGs, the acronym he coined for "big hairy audacious goals." I support this idea and have helped many brands craft BHAGs that their entire companies could embrace and be motivated by. But sometimes, we are not quite ready for BHAGs. What we need are baby steps in that daring direction. I guess you could call them BSITDDs. Most of us can relate to Bill Murray's character in the movie *What About Bob?* when he tries desperately to teach himself new behaviors by continually muttering to himself, "Baby steps, baby steps, baby steps" as he takes minuscule actions in the right direction. Little victories motivate us. Little victories are often just what we need to celebrate as brand leaders. Bite-size breakthroughs can often lead to bigger victories.

A newsletter came across my desk recently with this unlikely tidbit in it about the Wright Brothers:

"It is probably not well known that in 1901 Wilbur and Orville Wright arrived at the conclusion that man would not likely fly during their lifetime. Their discouragement came in response to being unable to control the up and down altitude movement called pitch, or the left right movement called yaw, of a glider which ended up spinning out of control. Fortunately, they went back to research and design. Their original design was good; yet its improvement is what made all the difference. They discovered that the addition of a moveable tail gave them the stability and control needed. The Wright brothers went on to make history in 1903 when Orville succeeded in a powered and sustained flight for 12 seconds and in 1904 when Wilbur succeeded in a 5 minute powered flight."

Three things struck me:

1. In 1901 they didn't think flying was possible, but only 24 months later they did indeed fly, thanks to the addition of a moveable tail.

2. The first flight victory was 12 seconds long.

3. Twelve months later the next victory was five minutes long.

Each of these seemingly little BSITDDs did inspire bigger breakthroughs. The Wright Brothers needed these little victories. Our brand leaders do as well..

This reminds me of a delightful book I read by Anne Lamott entitled *Bird by Bird: Some Instructions on Life and Writing.* I think it should be required reading prior to all goal setting. Lamott tells the story of her brother, a ten-year-old, who had a report due the next day, even though it had been assigned three months prior. He was immobilized by the task at hand when her father sat down with him and said, "'Bird by bird, buddy. Just take it bird by bird.'"

Where in your brand action plan could you benefit from some bird-by-bird encouragement?

Professor Rosabeth Moss Kanter calls it the "15 minute competitive advantage." In her *HarvardBusiness.org* blog she advocates "changing in short fast bursts rather than waiting for the breakthrough that transforms everything. If every proverbial 15 minutes, you learn something and incorporate it into the next speedy step, you'll continue to be ahead. And, a few time periods later, transformation will be underway."

This is so true; sometimes we need to gain the momentum of BSITDDs before we can see how the BHAGs can happen. Kanter goes on to say that these bite-size breakthroughs are often easier to sell. She advises, "Here are some characteristics of innovations most likely to succeed at gaining support: they are trial-able, divisible, reversible, tangible and familiar. In addition they fit prior investments, they are congruent with future direction and they have positive publicity value." Now think about the last thing your brand dared to do (whether related to people, products, services or process). How did it go? Did it actually happen? What were the unplanned lessons?

Unplanned lessons

Unplanned lessons are the exact opposite of lesson plans, those neat and tidy curriculum plans teachers try to follow until the students show up and things go awry. If we dare to review our actions, we often learn more from things that don't quite go the way we hoped than things that do. In a *BusinessWeek* article entitled "Radio Flyer Learns from a Crash," Thomas Schlegel, vice-president for product development at Radio Flyer shared his thoughts on a product launch that was halted. After months of development and lots of production time and dollars, Schlegel scrapped it. "It didn't live up to Radio Flyer standard," he said. According to the article, "his boss, Robert Pasin, CEO, told Schlegel failure was OK as long as the company learned from it." Radio Flyer is now "developing what Schlegel describes as an 'autopsy without blame,' in which everyone involved in the development of a product discusses four questions: What went well on the project? What didn't go well on the project? What did we learn? And, what are we going to do next?"

Author James Joyce gives us a new perspective on unplanned lessons: "A man of genius makes no mistakes. His errors are volitional and are the portals of discovery." Bravo to Radio Flyer. It made discoveries and acted on its volitional errors!

John Vitek, president and CEO of Saint Mary's Press, recently took an aggressive personnel risk. In the end, it turned out not to be the right fit for the organization. "In some ways it was one of the most disastrous decisions I made," says Vitek, "but also a decision that led to a big 'lesson learned.' In hindsight, while this hire did not seemingly fit our corporate culture long-term, the unplanned lesson I learned in all this was that our organization was indeed in need of change and resilient enough to bounce back from this error. Our team is more united than ever and with the right leadership recently just launched a new product that normally takes 12 or more months in less than one month."

I know it *used* to be a common practice for many multi-channelers to take the time to have strategic post-mortem conversations evaluating a season's results by sales channels (retail, online, and catalog) and by customer segments. Product visual boards would be created and the nuances of what worked and what didn't would be discussed along with promotional strategies and competitive tactics and offerings. In today's attention-deficit business culture, where everyone is chasing the next new thing, I'm afraid these important cross-departmental meetings have morphed into line item reports read individually and acted upon in silos. The subtle underlying threads of what didn't work do not get fully analyzed and the real failure of this short cut is that similar mistakes get made again (and possibly again).

I am a proponent of serious, slow talk (like the Slow Food, Slow Travel and Slow Christmas movements!) post mortems where true learning and insights can occur. I have both led and participated in these with my clients and they work and are worth it. Stop and think time. Concentrated focus on the previous season's happenings both for your brand and your customers' experience with your brand. Free flow of information. Open agenda. Robust conversations. Potential surprise endings.

Have you dared to look back? Where can you slow down and take time to better understand and collaboratively converse about your brand *faux pas?*

The f— word

I want to talk about the f— word. Not *that* f— word of course, but one that perhaps conjures up just as many emotionally negative connotations: **Failure**. We don't like to talk about failure. We don't like to admit that it could happen to us or that it *has* happened to us. We even think we might just bring it on by talking about it. We remember the shock of seeing a grade school teacher slash our tests with red wrong marks. We might have even gotten an F once or a D, or even a C- that felt like an F. We try to forget about failure as quickly as possible.

For some among us, even a B+ can feel like failure. Author Anne Lamott once gave a commencement address that *Salon.com* reprinted entitled "B+ is Just Fine." She says, "I was 35 years old when I finally got that B+'s are a good grade."

I know just what she means. I suffered from the same curse throughout most of my academic life, until a kind and recovering perfectionist helped me overcome this in college. Sister Peggy Albert, PhD, OP, now president, Siena Heights University, told me her story. While she was working diligently on her master's degree and trying hard to be a perfect student, one of her professors told her that all the work she had prepared for his particular class would earn her a B. She was allowed to do additional work if she wanted to earn an A. Sister Peggy knew that if she didn't do the extra work, this would be the only B on her entire graduate school transcript. She thought long and hard about it but she decided intentionally to live with the B to show herself that she did not always have to be perfect. "I was so happy I chose the B," she told me, "because it was a life lesson for me. I wasn't a different person because I got a B." So, as hard as it was for her, Sr. Peggy learned her lesson about the futility of perfectionism and then she taught it to me. It was one of my most valuable unplanned MBA lessons. I now teach it to my clients. "Strive for excellence, not perfection," says *Life's Little Instruction Book* author, H. Jackson Brown Jr. Perfection can kill a brand because it can paralyze it.

In the business world, instead of acknowledging failure, we often focus on praise. Who doesn't love hearing customer raves? "We love doing business with you." "Your service is excellent." "Thank you for going the extra mile." "I love your products." These are the words that bring a smile and a confidant nod to every business leader and are the ones passed around in company meetings when customer feedback is solicited. "We're doing great," we're told and we're soon on to the next topic. But, if this is *all* you are paying attention to as a brand leader, you are failing your brand. You are failing to seize the power of failure.

Recently, at two unique strategic planning sessions for two

different clients in entirely distinct industries, I diagnosed too much brand perfectionism in their organizations. I could tell they were all Type A, driven types who hated getting any red marks on their papers, both in school or in the office. They played it too safe. Their neat and tidy product development efforts were getting in their way. All the organizational process bureaucratic *i*'s were dotted and *t*'s crossed, but they were still missing the mark.

While these processes *once* served them well, they didn't any more. Products were late. Competitors were beating them to market. Costs were rising. Each product had to be so buttoned up before they released it that they lost both market share and profitability to more agile, less risk-adverse companies. Even more sadly, they left the customer entirely out of the loop in creating new products, so they missed a critical feedback tool that could have helped them hone their offerings. As internal experts, they thought they had to have all the answers themselves. They were used to getting straight A's. But getting an A+ in perfectionism can actually hinder your learning. Learning to let go and invite customers into your brand is the wonderful new work of today's brand leaders. Dare yourself.

I like Tim Littleton's attitude. As president and CEO of CHEFS, he makes a lot of courageous decisions. Some work, some don't. He explains it this way, "The luxury we have as direct marketers is the ability to constantly fail, but these failures help us hone in more precisely on what's more likely to succeed. We are instilled with the discipline of testing which allows for measured risk taking. Most tests, whether it is lists, creative, or merchandise may fail, but it's the winners that pay the bills and build the brand. If every new thing we try succeeds then we're not taking enough risk."

Brands need to embrace all aspects of failure at all levels of the organization, from taking the kind of risks that could lead to failure to encouraging employees and customers to talk about when the brand has let them down, to conducting thorough and honest assessments of what isn't working and why. It is only in a culture of failure acceptance that real success can happen. Writer Samuel Beckett encourages us with these words: "Go on failing. Go on. Only next time, try to fail better."

So, as brand leaders, how do we fail better? Here are a few suggestions.

Check your Branson meter

Many adjectives have been used to describe Richard Branson, but he describes himself by what he's not. "I'm not the sort of person who fears failure." I like that about him. It is a rare quality. In his latest business memoir, *Business Stripped Bare,* he acknowledges that real "failure is not giving things a go in the first place. . . I've learned more from people who have tried and faltered than from the charmed people for whom success came easy." So, how do you view failure? Do you go to great extents to avoid failure or do you purposefully push yourself (your brand, your team, your department) out of your comfort zone to take risks?

IBM founder Tom Watson operated by his own risk meter and was quoted as saying: "Would you like me to give you a formula for success? It's quite simple, really. Double your rate of failure. You are thinking of failure as the enemy of success. But it isn't at all. You can be discouraged by failure—or you can learn from it. So go ahead and make mistakes. Make all you can. Because, remember that's where you find success."

Jeffrey Katzenberg, chief executive, DreamWorks Animation SKG was interviewed in the *The New York Times* about another important aspect of failure. He said, "If you don't make failure acceptable, you can't have original and unique. And so in a world today that punishes, brutally punishes, any of us for failure, it's the single most important quality that I think we work so hard to provide for our 2,000 employees, the understanding that they are expected to take risks."

In a recent industry talk Rob BonDurant, VP of marketing for Patagonia, said simply "Patagonia is an experiment." (Read more about this "experiment" in founder Yvon Chouinard's business memoir, *Let My People Go Surfing*.) Kevin Churchill, the company's Director of Merchandising elaborated on this: "We are encouraged to take risks and not be afraid to fail. This is a company of surfers, climbers, risk takers. It's okay to fail at Patagonia; just have a contingency plan!" Even though Patagonia accepts that it will have some "misses," Churchill admits that misses are not as good as hits, but to think every enterprise will be a hit is what he calls a "gravity-defier."

So what is your brand's Branson Meter? Are you willing to jump in and make mistakes or are you possibly paralyzed by perfectionism? Ray Kroc, founder of McDonald's, pulled no punches: "If you're not a risk taker, you should get the hell out of business."

Welcome to the School of Hard Knocks

Hopefully, mistakes happen and they are a natural part of your brand's DNA. The real mistake is thinking your brand or company is "too big to fail" or, as Malcolm Gladwell wrote in a *New Yorker* article this year, "the psychology of overconfidence." Jim Collins also addresses this dynamic in his latest book, *How the Mighty Fall*. Collins' term is the "hubris born of success." There are warning signs all around us about the little guys winning big battles (just one example: Netflix taking on Blockbuster and now Redbox taking them both on! Who's next?), but many brand leaders still fail to look up and out. When brand leaders pay attention only to the positive feedback from their customers, they assume they are doing everything right. They get a bit arrogant about their competitive positioning. They think it is theirs forever. Wishful thinking is not part of the School of Hard Knocks curriculum.

In the School of Hard Knocks, stories of failure are welcomed. They are sought after, not hidden in the back of company drawers, hoping never to be noticed. They are analyzed and they become the catalysts of corrective action plans.

Award-winning American choreographer, Twila Tharp, writes in *The Creative Habit: Learn It and Use It for Life* about a benefit of failure: "I don't mean to romanticize failure, to parrot the cliché 'If you're not failing, you're not taking enough risks,' especially if that view 'liberates' you to fail too often. Believe me, success is preferable to failure. But there is a therapeutic power to failure. It cleanses. It helps put aside who you aren't and reminds you who you are. Failure humbles."

Does your brand ask both their employees and customers how they can be better served? Or where the brand has let them down? Are there any "work arounds" in the brand experience that make doing business with you difficult?

Target, a highly successful brand that often gives its biggest competitor a run for its money, once surveyed its customers as they exited the store. "Where are you going next?" it asked. "What *didn't* we have that you need to go elsewhere for?" In these interviews, it discovered that many of its middle-America-mom customers were headed to places like Hobby Lobby or Michaels for craft supplies. With this first-hand knowledge, it decided to take a calculated risk and add a craft department to its stores. The risk paid off. Target didn't think it had all the answers, nor was it afraid to take a risk with a new product category. Rather, it discovered what philosopher Leo Buscaglia believed to be true: "We seem to gain wisdom more readily through our failures than through our successes. We always think of failure as the antithesis of success, but it isn't. Success often lies just on the other side of failure."

Like Branson, my husband is not afraid of failure. I've learned a lot from his boldness in taking on new adventures. He tries things. He takes risks. He pushes me to do the same. If they don't work out, he simply sees it all as part of the adventure. The double black diamond ski runs he tackles have names like Widow Maker and Free Fall and Pin Ball and Adios. Mine, on the other hand, are light blue runs called Yellow Brick Road and Little Queen and School Marm and Peanut. I'm learning to be more Dean/Branson-y.

Dean has a large red ink stamp in his office that spells out the word WRONG in about inch-high letters. It's an intimidating word but one that we must make part of our vocabulary as naturally and easily as the  word RIGHT is. We miss a lot when we are or think we are always right. Author Joseph Chilton Pearce notes, "To live a creative life, we must lose our fear of being wrong." The book *How Starbucks Saved My Life* is really a treatise on this topic. It's the story of how Michael Gates Gill, former advertising executive at J. Walter Thompson, comes to terms with all the ways he's failed and the things he's been wrong about. He finds that true success often happens by listening to and living with our errors.

What is your brand doing to create some type of "failure feedback loop" to listen to and live with your errors? Don't be afraid of what you'll find; rather, think of it as a chance to learn and grow and potentially broaden your brand's horizons.

Another f—— word

Fired is the other f—— word I want to talk about. We think it's one of the worst things that can happen to us. It's not. It actually can be one of the most freeing. There are countless stories of people who were let go only to go on to fulfill dreams that never would have been possible if they were still chained by their golden handcuffs. Being fired is not the worst thing that can happen to your career. Being stuck in a role that does not feed your soul is. If we are lifeless, our brands become lifeless.

Jeffrey Kaztenberg believes that being fired from Disney "was one of the most difficult and painful and ultimately most valuable lessons" of his career. In *The New York Times* interview he said, "I genuinely loved my time at Disney, every day of it. But ultimately it was like getting pushed out the door, from the top of the building, and someone said, 'You better spread your wings if you want to see whether you can fly.'"

So fired can mean fly. Fired can mean freedom. And fired can mean new perspectives. Both Andy Grove, former CEO at Intel, and Andrea Jung, chairman and CEO at Avon, benefited from an exercise of "Pretend you were fired and got brought back in new. What would you do?" As reported in *US News & World Report,* Jung asked herself, "Can I be humble enough to destroy my own thinking of the last five years and recreate it as if I were a brand-new hire? The thing is, you're not new. You're taking out the same people you put in. Being able to reinvent yourself personally as a leader is just as important as reinventing the company and its strategy."

These brand do-overs happen in every industry. Pepsi went through a "creative destruction" under CEO Massimo D'Amore, not so quietly called "The Big Bang." Dell and Starbucks founders, Michael Dell and Howard Schultz, respectively, took second stints at the helm, taking their companies into uncharted brand territory when their visions stalled and fell to competitive pressures. Sam Walton's eldest son, Rob Walton, knows that do-overs are part of every brand strategy. "I learned from my dad that change and experimentation are constants and important. You have to keep trying new things."

Does anything need a do-over in your brand? What might be holding you back from acting more boldly? What if you were indeed fired, but then re-hired? What's the first thing you'd do?

Intentional stopping

Before I start brand conversations with my clients, I often share this *New Yorker* cartoon:

We pause. We breathe. We realize it's been a long time since we made the time to stop and think. The business world is a constant green **go go go** light.

It was while I was on a sabbati-

"It sort of makes you stop and think, doesn't it."

cal that I really began to appreciate the word **stop**. It literally almost hit me on my head. Dean and I were in Slovenia and he was on a three day international KTM adventure bike rally all over the rugged Julian Alps. I had three glorious days of retreat by myself in the rural town of Kobarid where, like the rest of the country, only Slovene was spoken. I did not speak Slovene. While my husband was thriving on a serious playful, no-English-spoken, challenging ride criss-crossing Austria, Italy, and Slovenia, I was content to conduct life like I might back home. I was looking forward to reading, writing, napping, and taking long walks through the countryside.

On my first morning, I found an outdoor café, ordered a pot of Earl Grey and proceeded to work on a book project. I had goals!

Soon after completing a few pages, I strolled to town, took in all
the strange signs and undecipherable messages along the roadside,
observed school children playing outside, managed to order a light
lunch, and then walked back to our accommodations. I found
a place in the sun on the veranda. Again I sat down to write. I
looked up and saw a large red American octagonal STOP sign (The
only sign in English around!). I know it had to have been there

before but I failed to notice it. I had
been too goal-oriented. I felt I was
being given a loud and clear message from this octagonal angel:
"Andrea, STOP! You may never
be in Slovenia again. Look up,
look out, drink in the unplanned
lessons of this country. Dare to
experience it all." When my husband arrived at our lodge after his
adventure, breathlessly but safely,
I had him take my picture next
to the sign with the Alps behind
him. It's my screensaver and a
perpetual reminder to STOP.

One of the key reasons failure happens in the business world
is because we forget to stop. We don't take the time to review and
discuss the intricacies of the failure we just experienced. Instead,
we either rush to cover it up, toss it into another silo, or move
forward rapidly with more go-go-go action before anyone really
notices. We need to embrace a culture of failure acceptance so
we can better understand what we need to stop doing.

I come from a long line of list makers. Perhaps you too are
a master list maker. There are many ways to make "to do" lists
from little post-it notes to sophisticated Franklin Covey systems
to online "Remember the Milk" programs. Mine is low tech and

modeled after something I saw my first boss, Ken Keoughan, use at the advertising agency he ran in Miami. Working first as an intern, then as a full-time employee, I learned a lot about both work and life from Ken. Twenty plus years later his time management method still works better for me than any patented or more complex system. On my desk is a yellow pad with a squiggly line down the middle. On one side is my work life list (prepare this client presentation, research that subject, implement these recommendations, send this proposal out, etc.) and on the other side of the squiggly is my personal life list (send care package to niece at college, arrange dinner party for Sarah's birthday, pack for sail trip, etc.) I keep these by month and week. I find the weekly list takes the pressure off the "it has to be done today" mentality and allows more flexibility for my energy level or travel schedule. The monthly list helps me set longer-term goals and provides an overall check on life and work balance. I like looking at both aspects of my life together. It provides a more integrated view and helps me not neglect one for the other. Work and Play. Play and Work. The two inform each other. These side-by-side lists also give me a chance to reflect on what I may need to stop doing.

Jim Collins is another list maker and has become famous for his "Stop Doing" lists. Early in his life, he too had a mentor, Professor Rochelle Myers, who cared about his personal success as well as his academic life. Despite Collins' high energy and achievements, she encouraged him to become more disciplined. To focus more. To do less of certain things. To stop doing other things all together. According to a reflection he wrote on his blog, she asked him questions like: What are you deeply passionate about? What are you are genetically encoded for—what activities do you feel just 'made to do?' What makes economic sense—what can you make a living at?

Collins, in his blog entry entitled "Best New Year's Resolution? A 'Stop Doing' List," writes: "Those fortunate enough to find or create a practical intersection of the three circles have the basis for a great work life. Think of the three circles as a personal guidance mechanism. As you navigate the twists and turns of a chaotic world, it acts like a compass. Am I on target? Do I need to adjust left, up, down, right? If you inventory your activities today, what percentage of your time falls outside the three circles? If it is more than 50 percent, then the stop-doing list might be your most important tool."

Reflecting on this advice, Collins continues: "Looking back, I now see Rochelle Myers as one of the few people I've known to lead a great life, while doing truly great work. This stemmed largely from her remarkable simplicity. A simple home. A simple schedule. A simple frame for her work. Rochelle spoke to me repeatedly about the idea of 'making your life a creative work of art.' A great piece of art is composed not just of what is in the final piece, but equally important, what is not. It is the discipline to discard what does not fit—to cut out what might have already cost days or even years of effort—that distinguishes the truly exceptional artist and marks the ideal piece of work, be it a symphony, a novel, a painting, a company or, most important of all, a life."

Building a brand that customers are passionate about is indeed an artistic endeavor. Those of you familiar with Collins's work remember that he took those three questions from his personal life and applied their wisdom to the business world. His best-selling book *Good to Great* is all about the intersection of those questions. "Greatness is not a function of circumstance. Greatness is largely a matter of conscious choice and discipline."

I don't believe Twila Tharp uses the phrase "stop doing lists," but she practices the principles. Here's how she explains it: "The better you know yourself, the more you will know when you are playing to your strengths and when you are sticking your neck out. Venturing out of your comfort zone may be dangerous, yet you do it anyway—our ability to grow is directly proportional to an ability to entertain the uncomfortable. And another thing about knowing who you are is that you know what you should not be doing, which can save you a lot of heartaches and false starts if you catch it early on."

Erik Buell, founder of Buell Motorcycle Company, made a conscious choice and a bold statement about a product that no longer fit its mission. He decided to stop manufacturing the Buell Blast. This entry-level beginner bike was not innovative or breakthrough enough and, according to *American Motorcyclist,* Buell is "rededicating itself to performance and innovation." So Erik Buell literally crushed the Blast for all to see on a video on the company's website. "Now we're back to what we really wanted to do, which is build real American sport bikes." No one will forget that visual symbol of a "to don't"!

Ben&Jerry's is another company that does not hide from its failures. In fact, in its typical irreverent fashion, it proudly shows them off in its Flavor Graveyard. Here's an example of the humorous gravestone for one of the flavors their customers just didn't love:

Ellen Kresky, creative director for Ben&Jerry's, told me "One of my favorite things about Ben& Jerry's is that we're not afraid to acknowledge our shortcomings or failures to consumers. Take our

Flavor Graveyard for example. We use it on our website, and you can actually go visit real tombstones at our Waterbury tour. The Flavor Graveyard features limericks to eulogize our flavor bombs. We even sell Flavor Graveyard t-shirts. A few years ago we had a contest to bring consumers' favorite flavor back from the dead for a limited time in scoop shops. A lot of us were secretly hoping that a flavor with a low gross margin would win so that consumers would benefit in more ways than one. And our wish came true. For me, this is an example of contrarian brand management. Projects like this help continue to build consumer love and trust, and manage to do that in an un-contrived way that stays true to our roots."

We can't figure any of this out if we don't stop. But when we stop long enough and look at our failures and our fears, we realize that there is yet another "f— word" we can embrace.

Fearless

Doug Hall, former master marketing inventor at Procter & Gamble and innovation researcher, taught me the acronym FUDs which stands for Fears, Uncertainties, and Doubts. I use this concept in most of my meetings to give brand leaders the freedom to say what is nagging at them about a particular decision or course of events on which we are about to embark. It's become a noun and one of my meeting norms as people say "I have a FUD about this," or "Does anyone else have a FUD about this?" FUDs allow us to pay attention to our intuition. They give us permission to take time for deeper conversation. FUDs are good for brand development. FUDs stretch us. They slow things down just enough to let us express our apprehensions and let others around the table debate the merits or problems entailed in a decision before we act. Handling FUDs in this healthy manner helps us recollect past actions and lessons learned from similar events. Talking about FUDs is a starting place for fearlessness.

Kathy Hecht, CMO, AG Interactive, a division of American Greetings, feels she is always pushing the FUD envelope with her team. "We are experimenting all the time—it's never really comfortable to take risks but I know it's the only way we'll grow. We call these tests into new waters 'duct tape marketing.' We try new things on our website, we tape it together as cheaply as we can, we see if it works, we repeat what works, we move onto the next experiment. We are always in test and learn mode."

Advertising great George Lois declared, "Only with absolute fearlessness can we slay the dragons of mediocrity that invade our gardens." *Daring. Stopping. Learning. Unlearning. Slaying.* These are all necessary action verbs in the vocabulary of bold brand leaders. By embracing failure and unpacking all that is involved in each brand faux pas, we become fearless. Our brands become less mediocre.

Dare Yourself and Your Brand Homework

So brand leaders, if you want to fail better, try a few of these exercises.

))) Failure report card

No doubt, we all like A+s. But sometimes our quest for A+s stops us from trying new behaviors. Creativity expert Gordon Mackenzie reminds us, "It's hard for corporations to understand that creativity is not just about succeeding. It's about experimenting and discovering." Conduct a failure evaluation for your brand and grade it on these subjects:

- How well does it embrace failure?
- How robust is its Branson-meter?
- When did it last examine its risk-taking portfolio?
- How well does it "listen to its errors"?
- Do departments share the lessons they've learned from their "brand blunders and bloopers" with other departments?
- Does it encourage FUDs?

(*Just an aside:* Anne Lamott ended that commencement speech by saying: "I just want to tell you one last thing. A B+ is a wonderful grade. . . . It's a wonderful grade." So, instead of being afraid to do this exercise because you know you won't merit an A, do it anyway. And remember, a B+ is a wonderful grade!)

))) Make waves

Sperry Top-Sider ran an ad for one of its new Aftersail sport

boots. The headline read, "Note To Self: Make Waves." Perhaps we all need this reminder. If your brand team were to write "a note to the brand," what would they write? What actions does your brand need to make more waves? Give your team members sticky notes and ask each person to write a note to the brand. Then read them aloud. What is the overall message? What are the FUDs about this message? Who is going to be Chief Wavemaker?

⋙ Make a list, check it twice

Right now, off the top of your mind, write down five things your brand needs to stop doing so it can be more effective and have more impact. Be daring and ask your customers a version of the same question: What are we doing as a company that is not of value to you? Or what item/service/policy/benefit do you never use and why?

⋙ Never say never

Christian retreat leader and author John Eldredge recently blogged about "things he would not be caught dead doing." I loved his honesty and humility. I was reminded how brands can sometimes be blinded to new directions simply because they always said "they would never be caught dead doing this or that." Back in the 1990s, I remember overhearing the leaders at Celestial Seasonings say they would never sell their tea at Walmart. Today, I smile when see shelves of their teas at Walmart. I believe it has become one of their largest accounts. I'm sure Howard Schultz thought he would never drink, let alone sell, instant coffee. Today, VIA Ready Brew is on Starbucks counters and part of the turnaround initiatives Schultz spearheaded to gain market share. What does your brand say it "would not be caught dead doing?" Why? Might it be time to take another look at some of those nevers?

Herald Your Brand

HAVE YOU EVER thought about your products or services as a herald for your brand? Dictionary.com gives us two meanings for the word herald. As a noun it is described as "formerly a royal or official messenger, especially one representing a monarch in an ambassadorial capacity during wartime." As a verb: "to give news or tidings of; to announce; proclaim; to usher in." I thought both were excellent descriptors of what a brand's products and services are meant to do for their customers. They serve as messengers and ambassadors; they usher in or announce what the brand is supposedly all about. How well do your products or services herald your brand? What messages are they sending? What kind of devotion are you giving to your "ambassadors"?

Many of us were taught the 4Ps of marketing (product, price, promotion, and place). Over my career, I have specialized in one of those Ps in particular: product. That P conjures up many other Ps in the art and craft of product making: positioning, packaging, pricing, personality, practicality, point of view, provocativeness, purpose, profitability, and promise, just to name a few. It is the right combination of these Ps in your product portfolio that leads to a propitious merchandising strategy.

Brands need propitious merchandising strategies now more than ever. An article from *The New York Times* reported that the recession has encouraged consumers to prefer experiences to things. A *New York Times*/CBS News poll found that many Americans are spending less on non-essentials including in stores and online. If we are honest with ourselves, most of the things we are trying to sell are nonessentials. Our job as brand builders is to make them essentials.

Walmart, the nation's largest retailer, understands this well and has positioned its executive leadership team to focus more intentionally on product. John Fleming, formally chief marketing officer of Walmart became its chief merchandising officer. I agree with Fleming's philosophy: "Think like a marketer, act like a merchant." With 84 percent of all households shopping at Walmart annually, Fleming and his team have their work cut out for them.

Throughout my 25 + -year career, I have worn the hats of both a marketer and a merchant so many times that it is hard for me to separate the two. My mentors have been people whose brains work double duty. This is how we think: "Why develop a fabulous new product if you don't first think about how it can be sold?" or "Why market to your customers the same old same old if your competitors are offering shiny and new?" I am constantly crossing the borders of the two disciplines and encourage my clients to as well. Maybe we need a whole new name for this role—the merchketeer!

Harvard Business School professor Clayton Christensen reminds brand marketers, "A product has a job to do for your customer." I remind my clients that their products (or services) either enhance their brand or detract from it. There really is no middle ground. It is the job of the merchketeer to be sure every product is "on brand," focuses on the customers' needs and desires, and creates a solution to make their lives simpler, easier, or better in some way. In addition, merchketeers add the surprise and magic that brands need to delight and wow their customers.

A merchketeer's tool box

So, just how is that done? I've developed ten practical and proven tools that merchants can use without breaking the bank. I couldn't work without these!

Collective Brilliance Tool

As we discussed in Chapter 5, this tool starts with taking some Stop and Think time. Turn off the smart phones and let all that is urgent on your desk and laptop wait a bit. Gather your best internal business brains in one room and just talk about your products. Invite all the merchants but include others connected to your products as well—creative folks, customer care folks, marketing and accountant types. They each "touch" the product line in their own way. Their various single beachball stripe perspectives are important! Take time for a real and in-depth conversation about your products. Actively listen to the insights and theories behind what's working and what's not. I've had the honor of leading these "collective brilliance conversations" with many of my clients. In all cases, the time invested was meaningful and worthwhile. Assemble an "internal beachball board of directors" and start a dialogue.

True North Identity Tool

First and foremost, be sure you know what business you are really in. Merchants are not just selling on-trend and brand-building products, they are selling something bigger. Sundance is selling more than artist-inspired jewelry, clothing, and home décor merchandise. Robert Redford, founder of Sundance, reminds his customers of this on his website: "To us, Sundance is and always will be a dream. What you see, smell, taste, and feel here is a dream being carefully nurtured. It is an area whose pledge is to people. What we offer in the form of art and culture, spirit and service, is homegrown and available to all." Fairytale Brownies is not just selling delicious brownies; it is selling "pure enchantment and "making the world a sweeter place." Before you create and offer more products or services, be sure you truly understand what all those products you are creating, sourcing and selling are really about. This mission becomes your brand's guiding compass for all you do.

Priceless and Thrive Tools

Believe it or not, sometimes brands struggle to find their true north. What is yours to do (versus your competitors') can get muddy as the competitive, customer, and economic climates change more rapidly than ever. Business writer Quentin Hardy speaks to this chaos, "Who can say what a competitor will be in a couple of years, in a world where Apple is a dominant force in music, Walmart is a doctor's office, and Amazon is your source for supercomputing?"

I created two tools that help companies get to the heart of what they are all about before they start thinking about the best products or services they can offer. The first uses a series of the long-running and famous MasterCard ads. My clients and I study several examples and we realize that Master- Card is really selling what's *under- neath* the products you can purchase with a credit card—what's truly price- less (time with your family, creating memories, celebrating someone) versus the actual golf clubs, or the vacation, or the fancy dinner out. I ask all the team members to pretend that their brand is going to conduct a campaign similar to MasterCard's. I

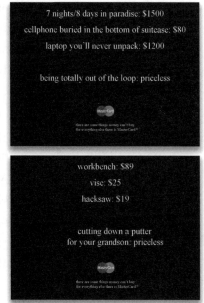

7 nights/8 days in paradise: $1500

cellphone buried in the bottom of suitcase: $80

laptop you'll never unpack: $1200

being totally out of the loop: priceless

MasterCard

there are some things money can't buy
for everything else there is MasterCard®

workbench: $89

vise: $25

hacksaw: $19

cutting down a putter
for your grandson: priceless

MasterCard

there are some things money can't buy
for everything else there is MasterCard®

ask them to follow that "1-2-3-Priceless" formula and to come up with ads and construct a tagline about "what money can't buy" regarding their brand. We read all of these and then we write down on a large white board all the priceless last lines.

This is an amazing exercise to help team members see and understand more clearly the emotional "product" they are selling. This is really their True North.

We stand for broccoli. For Pilates. And dental floss.
We believe in the treadmill and its siblings StairMaster, and elliptical. In SPF-30 we trust. We stand for seat belts and stopping HIV. And we believe fruit makes a wonderful dessert. We have faith in optimism. In laughter as medicine as well as penicillin. And we pledge allegiance to one nation, indivisible with resistance and cardio for all. We believe in physical therapy, psychotherapy, even music as therapy. All hail cold turkey, the gum, and the patch. We're anti-addiction. Pro-antioxidant. And have never met a vegetable we didn't like. We believe there is art to medicine as well as science. And we believe health isn't an industry, it's a cause. We are Kaiser Permanente and we stand for health. May you live long and thrive.

KAISER PERMANENTE. thrive

I also conduct a similar creative exercise based on the Kaiser Permanente "Thrive" campaign. This is an ingenious copy-heavy ad that, like the MasterCard campaign, gets underneath the fact that Kaiser is actually selling health insurance. The ads talk about what Kaiser Permanente as a brand stands for (we are pro . . . , we believe in . . .) as well as what they are against (we're anti- . . .). It believes good health is a cause, not an industry and it isn't until the very end that you realize who it is and what it is "selling." In this case, I encourage my clients to pretend that they are launching a similar campaign and have them create their own "Thrive" ad. We tally up all the things they compose in columns, connect the emotional dots, and have a pretty clear picture about what the brand is really all about.

Catholic worship music source, OCP, in Portland, Oregon, embraced this exercise with gusto. Here's what John Limb, president of OCP, said, "It really did get us to the heart of OCP's brand. What's key to our brand is the 'experience of worship' that results from folks using our music and worship materials. We're aware of this, not only because of the feedback from our customers, but because many of us are also pastoral musicians and have had the same experience. Tapping into that experience is a far more effective way of capturing what it is that OCP does. It's not really about the songbooks or the CDs we publish, but rather, it's about the lives that are changed as a result. Doing the 'Thrive' exercise was certainly enjoyable, inspiring, and invigorating. The focus and positive energy that resulted helped us to make the necessary changes in the months that followed."

Brand Dictionary Tool

What seven words best describe your brand? (Not your tagline, although let's double-check that those brief words are brand-clarifying too.) What adjectives would your customers use to describe your brand? Now compile those two lists and see if they synch up. Is your brand perception the same internally and externally? Next, take those words and write definitions for them for your brand. Document this! Most times, the adjectives that describe your brand will also describe your products.

I once worked with a company that perceived its brand as "homey." Some merchants thought "homey" meant "cozy" and "down-to-earth" whereas others surprised us and thought homey meant "Martha Stewart" and "sophisticated." We had to spend some time on the word "homey" until we had a definition that articulated this brand's particular perspective and that all the product development folks could agree upon.

This exercise led to some excellent results for one of my clients. I had spent an imaginative day onsite with members of the Boston Proper merchandising and creative teams, brandstorming their brand descriptors. The busyness of running and executing the business took over and the brand descriptors were left on a shelf until Sheryl Clark, the new CEO and president of Boston Proper, came on board. Here's how she related the experience: "When I came to BP I spent the first few weeks going through all its customer research, data and surveys, and a branding project the company had commissioned. The branding project had excellent information; the problem was that it wasn't being used. Working with my CCO, we turned the branding deck of words into a *Boston Proper Brand Book*, a usable guide for both internal and external users that explained in a creative and exciting format the Brand Objective, the Brand Purpose, a description of Boston Proper using five key words, who the Boston Proper Woman was, and last and most important, the product filters used to make our merchandise selection. All the words went back to a picture that was Boston Proper's creative product expression of that word. We made hundreds of copies of our Brand Book; we took everyone in the company through it and each employee got a bound copy to live by. We took all our key vendors through it and used it in our hiring process. Mine sits on my desk and not a day goes by that I don't use it. We start all our key meetings with our Brand Book and by staying true to the brand attributes we stay true to the Boston Proper customer. She lives in the pages of that book!"

Clark advises, "If you are spending money on a project you must understand how to incorporate the work into the culture and DNA of the company." In other words, use it or lose it!

James Avery also uses a brand dictionary of sorts as a clarifying tool. Here's how the company describes it on its website:

"The Avery Look is nothing new. It has no pretense of being so. It tries to assimilate and reflect many cultures and the art of those cultures. One might say that The Avery Look is an attempt to embody an insight into all ages and periods of artistic achievement. It is difficult to define. However, some of the attributes and values from The Avery Look have grown into a company philosophy. Each piece of jewelry should pass the tests of Simplicity, Integrity, Meaning and Universality. These four 'founding values' are deeply carved into wood planks hanging prominently on the solid stone walls of our present-day Design Studio. It's a constant reminder of what we believe."

Board of Customers Tool

If there is collective brilliance within your brand's four walls, just imagine what exists outside them! In a perfect world, merchants would hang out with customers on a daily basis and in this casual mingling would discuss all sorts of product-related issues. In a perfect world, customers would be at office meetings when important merchandising decisions are being made. Since these scenarios usually are not possible, merchants need to create their own "on call" (or email) board of customer advisors. This representative sampling of real life customers and users of the brand's products are instrumental in being a true sounding board for help on issues like pricing, color selections, fabrics, and so forth. These customer conversations can provide merchants with authentic "emotional intelligence" about product decisions.

Another one of my clients told me how this emotional intelligence influenced a new venture. Diana Larson Stuart, Hallmark Properties creative director shared this with me: "When extending or expanding your product line, dig deep for what consumers expect from you and what differentiates you as a brand. Consider consumer need and use, design style, presentation, and even meaning. We always believed that flowers were a natural extension of the Hallmark brand idea for consumers. But when we added an additional layer of meaning to our bouquets through words and symbols incorporated into the floral and vase design— allowing consumers to send the kind of message they expected from Hallmark—we saw sales jump."

These "boards of customers" can be formal or informal, a small group or large. Bridal gown company Priscilla of Boston recently ran a limited time social media campaign asking its customers to act as a board. The campaign asked "How does Priscilla of Boston inspire you?" and invited its customers to create photo collages of gowns that inspired them and tell the stories of why.

Customer Profile(s) Tool

Sometimes things just go your way. During the 2008 Summer Olympics, women's clothier Chico's received a sprinkling of

merchandising fairy dust. Debbie Phelps, mom of eight-time gold medalist Michael Phelps, was televised wearing Chico's outfits event after event as she cheered her son to victory. Chico's received Ms. Phelps' permission to showcase her selections on its website. Soon afterwards, it offered her an endorsement. Why? Debbie Phelps, a 57-year-old, successful school principal epitomized the Chico's customer. I have no doubt the merchants at Chico's call their ideal customer "Debbie."

The merchants at Appleseed's, another clothing company targeting a similar baby boomer female, call their customer "Kate." While Kate is not an Olympic mom, she is a real-life composite picture of their customer based on the team's qualitative and quantitative research. A well-known lingerie company uses the names of the characters from *Sex and the City* as its persona descriptors.

Most companies do not have just one customer segment; they have several. It is important to have a thorough visual and word picture of each of your customer segments. By continually "picturing" your customers in all that you do, your brand starts to make decisions through their lens. What would Debbie think about this tote? What would Kate wear this spring season? As a side note, I believe all departments should make use of these tools, not just merchandisers and marketers. The more all employees truly "get" their customers, the more effective brand ambassadors they can all be and the more an organizational beachball culture will be cultivated.

Have you "named" your customer(s)? What does he or she look like? Why not create a word and visual collage of your customer(s) and share it with all your team members.

Product Rock-Star Boards Tool

Many companies generate stacks of reports or spreadsheets of product metrics and status. Often these analytics are underused, scanned quickly, or forgotten all together. I find that creating product rock star boards help turn a plethora of numbers into interesting stories. The merchants at Boston Proper did just that. While creating product visual boards was always a part of their thorough review process, the merchandising department took it a step further. The merchants looked at their top performing products across three key metrics and created a visual board for its "product rock stars." These products sold lots of units, brought in revenue, were brand enhancers, and contributed meaningfully to the bottom line. These products will drive line extensions and potential category development.

Do you know which products are your rock stars?

Product Fit Chart Tool

Upon clarifying both your brand's true north, (or your unique selling proposition—USP) and your brand adjectives, it is time to create a product fit chart using those adjectives and other descriptors (price point ranges, functionality, themes, and so on) that will become your merchandising GPS. This is one of the most effective planning tools I've used. It instills objectivity in choosing products. No longer is the "merchant's favorite" or the "vendors' great deal" the only criteria for decision-making. The fit chart enables the product selection process to become a more strategic and systematic vetting plan for the whole department. It generates excellent conversations among merchants and it guides the team to make brand-enhancing decisions versus brand-detracting ones.

Exclusively Weddings did just that when Cindy Marshall became president of the ecommerce division of Pace Communications, its parent company. I led an all day "Stop and Think" meeting with her team in order to create a product fit chart that would guide this brand as the company started to expand in different areas. Marshall comments, "When building a product assortment for any brand you need to be extremely clear on what your unique selling proposition is and why customers will want to buy from you. At Exclusively Weddings we focus on offering our customers, primarily brides, everything they need to plan their wedding with the exception of the dress, the jewelry, and the venue. We are primarily an online store so we focus on offering an assortment that doesn't need to be touched in person, like a wedding gown. When planning our product assortment, we evaluate each item to determine if we should carry it by answering the following questions:

- Does it meet our product fit chart requirements of high quality, value, personalized, category expert, keepsake, a collection, stylish traditions, tasteful, exclusive, and easy to use and explain?

- What is the price point and do we already have too many items in this range? Are we missing items in a certain price range?

- How does our product compare in quality and style to our competition?

- Are we giving our brides something new to select from or will this product cannibalize our existing product line?

- Are we giving our brides too many choices? Have we

selected the best items that are in the 'good, better and best' categories?"

Product fit charts are clarifying and centering. I have helped all sorts of companies create these, ranging in scope and product types from Exclusively Weddings to Celestial Seasonings to Abbey Press to Ben & Jerry's. Every brand needs one whether launching a new product line or refining an existing one.

Does your brand have a product fit chart?

"The Enemy's" Product Fit Chart Tool

Every brand has its own version of Goliath. What competitor would you like to slay? Knowledge is power. Spend time reviewing your competitors' products, first through your own fit chart. How many of "theirs" do you carry? Why? Are you "borrowing" their true north? Are they borrowing yours? How much customer confusion are you generating? Take a look at some cooking brands or office supply brands. You'll see little differentiation! Next, try to create your competitors' fit chart (or their "Priceless" or "Thrive" campaigns!). Not only will your merchants gain greater insights into their "Goliaths," but this tool will also help in your own product vetting process. Keep the competitors' fit charts as a handy sidebar reference to your own as you struggle with certain product selections. Be sure the products you select are yours to sell, not your competitors!

Checklist Tool

There are checklist people and there are non-checklist people. I've always been the former and found that checklists serve me well. I like to use lists when creating, sourcing, and selecting products and then again when selling those products across multichannels. Therefore, I was thrilled when an article in *The New Yorker* confirmed the importance of this practice. Surgeon and writer Atul Gawande wrote an essay called "The Checklist" with the subhead "If something so simple can transform intensive care, what else can it do?"

It was a fascinating story about how Dr. Pronovost, a critical care specialist, and his colleagues studied the measured practices of pilots and implemented simple checklists to prevent intensive care infections. The checklists worked. Lives were saved. Infection rates were down dramatically. What seemed silly at first actually helped "establish a higher standard of performance." Dr. Gawande's essay has since been expanded into a book entitled *The Checklist Manifesto: How to Get Things Right.* Like the product fit chart, a "selling" checklist can be implemented by the merchants but then shared with the creative team as a practical barometer for double and triple-checking that everything has been done to ensure that product (category, theme) sells as well as possible. Why bother investing in product development if that same energy isn't given to make the product enticing online, on the page, or in the store?

As your brand continues to face challenges in the competitive, customer, and economic arenas, why not face those challenges squarely and confidently with the use of these strategic merchandising tools?

Purposeful subtraction

I spend a lot of time with brand leaders helping them unpack words. I find it imperative to be sure everyone around the table understands the nuances involved in their brand's descriptors and fit chart adjectives. If someone is operating with one definition of the word "trendy" and someone else understands it a bit differently—from nuances as potentially different as "on trend" to "trend-setting"—there is a good chance that decisions will be made using potentially conflicting criteria.

Matthew E. May made me think about a word differently in his book, *In Pursuit of Elegance: Why the Best Ideas Have Something Missing.* When you hear the word "elegance" all sorts of brand names come to mind: Jaguar, Chanel, Tiffany & Co., Cartier, Christian Louboutin, Rolex, Four Seasons, Waterford, and others. So when you open this book, you think you might be tackling a book about luxury branding. However, this is not at all what the author was talking about.

The concept of elegance as defined by May is all about "being two things at once: unusually simple and surprisingly powerful." He continues, "One without the other leaves you short of elegant. And sometimes the 'unusual simplicity' isn't about what's there, it's about what isn't. At first glance, elegant seems to be missing something." He goes on to tell us that "elegance cuts through the noise, captures our attention and engages us. The point of elegance is to achieve maximum impact with minimum input. It's a thoughtful, artful subtractive process focused on doing more and better with less."

So, bottom line, less is more. Or more specifically, doing the *right* less can produce the *right* best. By his way of thinking, elegance isn't reserved for high-end luxury brands. Elegance can apply to fast food. May writes, "Elegance isn't about being hoity-toity. It's not about lofty concepts and grand designs. It's not about beauty or grace, or anything to do with aesthetics—ugly is okay. Elegance is about something much more profound. It's about finding the *"aha!"* solution to a problem with the greatest parsimony of effort and expense. Creativity plays a part. Simplicity plays a part. Intelligence plays a part. Add in subtlety, economy, and quality, and you get elegance."

I find his re-definition of the word elegance very helpful. Purposeful subtraction. It makes you stop and think about the hyperactivity that we can all slip into unintentionally. It reminds me of the purple kitchen colander on my work desk that I use as a visual to remind me of the power of sifting. For me, this purple metal colander, which is really meant for draining potatoes or pasta, is a symbol that just because everything *could* be done, doesn't mean that everything *should* be done. I need to be a constant sifter and editor of all my business activities. It's a tool that I use with my clients as we evaluate all their brand activities and product opportunities and discuss what really will matter most to their customers.

Using May's definition, just how elegant is your brand's product line? Whether you are selling insurance, oranges, shoes, office supplies, high-tech equipment, or children's clothing, the art of elegant merchandising is a discipline worth pursuing. However, before you can craft products or services that truly "cut through the noise, capture customers' attention and engage them," you must be a diligent observer of your customers' behavior. In my experience, this is one activity that brands need to increase.

How much time are you spending in direct customer contact? One sure way to increase your brand's merchandising intelligence is by increasing your customer intelligence. The elegant company examples that May cites are all active anthropologists of their customers' lives in their respective product categories. This is how they find the "elegant solutions." This is how they know which features are "too many" and which ones are "just right."

Michele Fortune, the vice president of product at DRG, a third-generation family business "celebrating home, family, and the creative spirit" discusses the necessity for customer attentiveness. "Years ago, after a senior management meeting, I went back to my office thinking, 'If only we would spend as much time listening to our customers as we do listening to ourselves,' and I have tried to make that the driving force of my efforts ever since. Let your customer guide you. While it is important for merchandisers to be trendsetters, I find the most important driving force to sustaining profitability is to effectively respond to customer's ever-changing needs. The key is to find a solution, and when possible, preemptively. Productive innovation, product enhancements, and extensions are often a direct result of customer communications in the form of selling reports, emails, complaints, and returns. Listen and respond with creative and elegant solutions."

Let's look at four "just right" simply elegant examples from the not-so-glamorous product categories of tea, socks, stationery, and kitchen utensils.

Tea Forté Cocktail Infusions

This brand caught my attention from its inception and it continues to evoke emotion ("I must have this!") and engage my senses. Founder Peter Hewitt had big dreams: "My original vision was modest, just to reinvent the entire tea ceremony, a centuries old tradition! I wanted to create a total sensory and emotional experience that was relevant to life today. I considered taste, smell, touch and, of course, visual presentation. I wanted to create a simple ceremony, a special moment to enjoy with family, friends or just by myself." And that he did with his gorgeous gift-worthy silken tea infusers and unusual Zen-like presentation pieces. What has impressed me lately though is the company's ability to bring that same sensibility and symmetry to another category in a unique way: cocktails. Tea Forté now has an amazing collection of cocktail infusions (like teabags for your spirits!), artisan cocktail glasses, and even a mixology set. The merchants at Tea Forté have mastered the art

of elegant merchandising. I can't wait to see what they do next!

LittleMissMatched Socks

This brand has always made the lowly sock an absolutely fun item. With its tagline, "Think Outside the Socks," LittleMiss-Matched continues to add whimsy and novelty to this category. These are socks that you don't want to keep in the drawer! Its holiday limited edition recently featured something called Kooky

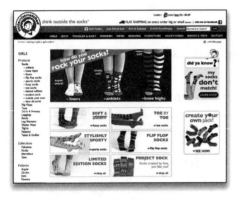

Socks, a pack of three knee high, double cuff socks that give the wearer 48 ways to match them up. Colorful, irresistible, and yes, kooky, LittleMissMatched subtracts boredom and conventionality from its category and serves up a great deal of creativity and ingenuity.

Crane's Greeting Card Caddy

Even though people may not be writing letters much these days, they still might take a minute to jot a note. Crane understands that it is now competing with the speed of email and the fun of social media. So it has developed a simple product that can sit beside its customers' workspace or tuck inside their desk drawers that makes sending a note quick and easy. Its Greeting Card Caddy doubles as a mini-organizer complete with a perpetual calendar for recording dates and twelve greeting cards. It's simple, accessible, contained, and a problem-solver for customers.

Pyrex Measuring Cups

If you've ever fumbled around your gadget drawer for the 1/3 cup measurer only to come up with the 1/4 cup and the little ring that used to hold all four together, this new product from Pyrex is for you. Pyrex solved the problem of separated measuring cups with an elegant solution: magnetized handles. It also redesigned the cup portion so they scoop and pour flour and sugar more easily. An everyday product with unusual simplicity.

In true BrandAbout fashion, why not use these examples to jump-start your own internal elegance discussion? What areas of your brand need a bit of sifting and editing? What products might be collecting a bit of "feature creep"? How can you and your team do some purposeful subtracting that will not only increase your merchandising intelligence but engage your customers more fully into your brand experience? Getting more elegant is creative, intentional work. Get busy getting more elegant before your competitors do!

Playing with the Ps

Even though we are all taught to mind our Ps and Qs, we sometimes forget. In this book, we've talked quite a bit about the importance of some Qs (like being a Questioner-in-Chief, cultivating a questioning mindset, and so forth). Now I want to shift the focus to the powerful Ps as they relate to your product development strategy: positioning, packaging, pricing, personality, practicality, point of view, provocativeness, purpose, profitability, presentation, and promise. These are some of the Ps that merchants arrange like puzzle pieces in crafting a strategic merchandising plan. From there, the individual items (or stock keeping units—SKUs) get fit together under categories, theme, price points, and other subclassifications until a wonderful customer experience is created.

Let's play with just one of those Ps for now and see how taking a little "Stop and Think" time can broaden our perspective on packaging. The effectiveness of this approach as a strategic merchandising and branding process plays out over and over again as I witness many companies borrow brilliance from different fields to make quantum leaps in innovations of their own. Let's wander through a few examples from various industries and see how some merchants have excelled in the often under-leveraged area of packaging.

The Power of a New Format: BelGioioso and Wipes, Wipes, Wipes!

Sometimes repackaging an existing product in a new formulation is all it takes to enliven a category and extend a product's usefulness. Take a look at the BelGioioso Unwrap and Roll Fresh Mozzarella Sheets. I first saw this eye-catching product innovation at the Fancy Food Show a few seasons ago. It made me squeal. As an Italian, I love mozzarella cheese in all forms, but a whole sheet? Sheer heaven! Packaging mozzarella in a new shape and size (like Pillsbury's refrigerated piecrust) gives customers everything they want: convenience and a chance to be creative in their own "inner Giada" ways.

Then there's the whole category of wipes. This packaging format has taken hold in many categories. What started out as repurposing the humble wash cloth became a superstar packaging format that has permeated every industry: ArmorAll car cleaning wipes, Swiffer floor cleaning wipes, Noxema facial wipes, Cutex nail polish remover wipes, Clorox disinfecting wipes, Pledge multi-surface wipes, Cutter insect repellent wipes, MD Mom's Baby Silk sunscreen wipes, Avon Skin-So-Soft wipes, and even full-body Fresh Body Bath wipes, the size of bath towels. This is just a quick top-of mind sampling!

Take a look at your best-selling product's existing format. Are there any ways to re-configure it that would delight your customers?

The Power of a Packaging Partner: Evian and Ford

The brand leaders at Evian knew it was time to give this bottled water company a bit of a packaging punch. They rolled out a new "Live Young" ad campaign and partnered with British designer Paul Smith for a limited edition, playful package that would garner new attention on the crowded beverage shelves. According to Jerome Goure, vice president of marketing for Danone Waters of America, Inc., "The Paul Smith Limited Edition 2010 bottle truly captures the new Live Young™ mindset that believes everything is possible and challenges the status quo. This third annual designer Evian bottle is a perfect addition to our current portfolio of products, and we're thrilled to include it in our collection."

Ford Motor Company has had long-standing partnerships with Eddie Bauer and King's Ranch. Both partners offer their Expedition customers a chance to showcase their personalities through these customized additions.

Are there any partnership opportunities that would enable you to dress up your existing products in a new way, offer your customers something more, and challenge your brand's status quo?

The Power of a Clever New Display: Sephora

Fashion forward companies like H&M and Sephora are used to reacting quickly to trends. Their customers crave up-to-the-minute fashion forward products and expect these brands to deliver

the goods, pronto! Sephora built the excitement of all that pent-up demand into its Runway Palette, a set of eye shadows, bronzers, and blush "created to make applying Fall's hottest runway looks easy and fun." The smart merchants at Sephora capitalized on two things: the clever naming of the product and also a perspicacious delivery of the product. The Runway Palette separates itself from other makeup collections because it packages the eye shadows and blushes in configurations that look like buttons and cable knit sweaters—a small but big detail that will certainly catch the attention of fashionistas!

Might your products benefit from some clever naming (or renaming)? Might you be able to deliver the benefits of your products in a new and provocative way that adds some buzz-worthiness?

The Power of the Leave Behind:
Life Is Good and Hobo International

Merchants don't often remember to save time and energy for the last and most memorable product component: the hang tag. Two companies that cater to two different audiences, Life is Good and Hobo International, both realize that the little extra storytelling that can be accomplished on something as small as a business card can be an important packaging component that differentiates their brands.

The Boston-based sportswear company, Life is Good, has double-sided thick paperboard tags that remind customers how the company got started and how it continues to "spread optimism worldwide" on one side while driving home its logo and tagline of "Do What You Like. Like What You Do." on the other.

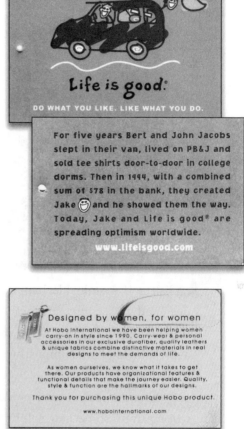

Hobo International, a leather and accessory "carry-on" brand, uses its card (slipped inside wallets and handbags) to connect more deeply with its customer base. "Designed by women, for women," states the card. "At Hobo International we have been helping women carry on in style since 1990. As women ourselves, we know what it takes to get there . . ." and then the tag adds, "Thank you for purchasing this unique Hobo product." Two different tactics, but one smart merchandising strategy: add one more engaging brand touchpoint to the purchase.

Is there a packaging component that would make your product become a better brand sales tool? How and where do you say "thank you" to your customers now? Is it meaningful? What if your hangtags were your Chief Merchant's business card with a note requesting feedback from your customers about product improvements?

The Power of Positioning Adjectives: Gardener's Supply Company

When you think compost, you don't often think pretty. And you wouldn't normally want to "display" your compost container. Juxtapositioning is a propitious merchant's tool to get customers to pay attention. And that's just what the smart merchants at Gardener's Supply Company accomplished by thinking about the practicality of a product's packaging when it developed its stylish and sustainable bamboo crock with removable pail. "We designed this compost crock for good looks and convenience" reads the selling copy. This product just might persuade those averse to kitchen composting by selling "pretty" right next to "practical."

What are some of your product "givens"? Is there any way you can mash up some new solutions and re-package your product to appeal to a new audience?

Maximizing the Power of Color: Fresh Produce Sportswear

This Boulder, Colorado-based women's apparel company is all about fresh fun clothes packaged in happy colors and comfortable cotton. Co-founders, Thom and Mary Ellen Vernon take color seriously and package it as an integral part of their brand. The beach-inspired palette with names like Citrus, Sangria, South Beach Blue, and Aqua Del Sol helps to position all its clothes as wearable art and evoke that sought-after vacation feeling. These colors are used not just on its clothes, but throughout its entire company as an integral brand component. Offices are painted in these colors, teams are named by these colors, and fashion shows revolve around these colors.

The impact of color is critical to brand marketing because color increases brand recognition by up to 80 percent, according to a Loyola University Maryland study. Brands spend a lot of time and energy packaging color in ways that become inseparable from their iconic products. Whether it's the red of Target's bull's-eye, the green of John Deere's tractors, the brown of UPS' fleet, boxes, and uniforms, or the all-encompassing orange at Home Depot, color is an important packaging asset that is often under leveraged.

Does your brand own a color? Can that color be made a more vibrant part of your merchandising platform?

As a merchant passionate about creating products customers love, I encourage you to use these examples as a springboard to start your own conversation on one of the Ps and see if they may inspire a bit of propitious merchandising for your next product development session. Tom Peters encourages us all to "do things that are gasp-worthy." I believe gasp-worthy things done right enhance your brand. Look up, look out, look about! Go on your own packaging, presentation, pricing, or provocative walkabout. Your brand deserves it!

Herald Your Brand Homework

Here are a few more exercises to encourage you to develop purposeful products that truly herald your brand.

〰️ Eat, pray, love

Marketer Jack Trout wrote the bible on positioning years ago. In an interview with *Women's Wear Daily,* he said: "Strong marketing campaigns in the 21st century are best built on pithy statements of what a brand represents, rather than flashy technology, a rush to social media or glib sloganeering." Trout firmly believes in the "power of a simple marketing message." I couldn't agree more.

In another attempt to get to your brand's true north and come up with your own unifying and simple marketing message (after trying the "Priceless" and "Thrive" exercises), try this: writer Elizabeth Gilbert brilliantly sums up the tale of her year long travels in three countries in the pithy title of her memoir *Eat, Pray, Love* (Eat representing her time in Italy, Pray her time in India, and Love her adventures in Bali). Pretend your brand is a story requiring a three-word title. What would it be and why?

⑅ Pop-up storybook

Remember Diane Ackerman's play analogy of a pop-up storybook in Chapter 1 (page 6)? I often compare the work of creating or recreating a brand to writing a compelling book

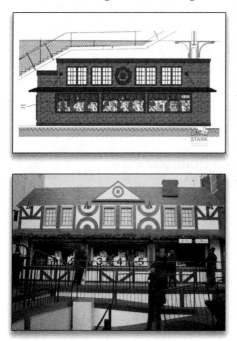

with many chapters, themes, and pages, all unified to tell one story. An integrated brand story is a must these days to capture both your customers' fleeting attention spans and their share of wallet and heart in your category. Brand stories provide the basis for that integration and a strategic and defining narrative for both your internal and external audiences. Without a brand story as a true north compass for all your strategic business activities, your brand can lose its soul.

Without making that story clear to your customers in all that you do, your brand can lose its competitive edge. Hopefully your brand story is rich and engaging, a virtual page turner for your customers bursting with a mix of old and new, grounded by a solid heritage but open to being O.P.E.N. to today's customers' changing lives and needs.

Pretend that your brand is a storybook and lay out your brand's central themes and stories. What pops? What stories need greater depth? What themes need more development? What is unclear to your readers (customers)? Create a visual of some type (a storyboard, a diorama, a scrapbook, an actual pop-up book—whatever!) to show where you'd like to take your brand next.

⫸ Please don't pass by the Ps

We've already established the importance of all the merchandising Ps: positioning, packaging, pricing, personality, practicality, point of view, provocativeness, purpose, profitability, presentation, and promise. Now create a checklist for your brand to use to ensure that these important Ps don't get passed over in your next product development planning cycle.

⫸ What's yours to do?

Mim Harrison, founding editor of Levenger Press shared this about individualizing your brand through herald products: "Exclusivity has long been a differentiator for Levenger, and one of the ways we've underscored this is through an exclusive line of books that we create ourselves. It's almost unheard of these days not to be able to find a book anywhere you look, so being able to say 'available only at Levenger' ups the desirability quotient. We've also been able to cross-pollinate the publishing arm and our product line on various occasions. For instance, we used the whimsical drawings of pigs by Sir Winston Churchill that were featured in one of the Churchill books we published as the basis for a sculpted bookend. Again, these items are only available through us." Clearly, the smart merchketeers at Levenger's know what products are theirs and theirs only.

Act like a merchketeer and go through your product line to purposefully subtract (use that purple colander if you must!) the products that are not yours after all. Line them up, talk about why these made the cut, and then create a Stop Doing list of the mistaken criteria. Post it. Use it.

7

Craft Your Brand

I THOUGHT of my dad when I read what William D. Green, chairman and CEO of Accenture, said in a *New York Times* interview: "I'm a proud plumber's son from western Massachusetts. In my family, working with tools is the highest honor. It isn't how many degrees you have. It's what you can do. So that had a big impact on me. What that says is, it doesn't matter what you look like, what you talk like, where you went to school, where you came from, any of that stuff. What matters is what you're capable of."

Well, I'm a proud electrician's daughter. Dad started as an electrical apprentice who over the course of an almost three-decade career (he died too early at age 48) eventually worked his way into a training and development career instructing teachers at a major steel company in Pennsylvania. When I was growing up, he often did electrical jobs for friends and neighbors on weekends and my sisters and I would accompany him as his "assistants." This meant we handed him tools (we would get quizzed on the differences between a flat-head screwdriver and a Phillips head) and generally stood around until he needed something. Our favorite part was eating our packed lunches with him like real on-the-job laborers.

I also remember making posters about Ohm's Law for the electrical trade class he taught at a vocational technical school. He

was in his mid-career teaching 17- and 18-year-old guys the nuts
and bolts of the electrical trade. (There were no women in his
classes, although this was the 1970s and there could and should
have been.) His was no easy course. My dad had a reputation
for being strict and had high requirements for his apprentices. I
remember his students coming to our house on various occasions
to ask my dad's advice on matters not at all electrical-related. He
mentored them in many areas of life. Like me, these young men
appreciated my dad and looked up to him.

In addition to creating the Ohm's Law posters, I recall going to
the Vo-Tech school with dad on Saturdays to see the progress being
made on the miniature house that the school's entire student body
was building. Dad's class was doing the electrical work; another
group had done the carpentry and the plumbers were up next. It
looked like a giant dollhouse to me. I was fascinated that this is
what some people did in school. It seemed so real and practical.
Beachball collaboration before I knew it!

My dad was first and foremost a coach and a teacher. He was
a practical man. He spent a great deal of time prompting me and
my three sisters to do more than what we thought we were capable
of—in school, on the track, and in life. Now I spend much of my
time prompting brand leaders in the same way. It's in my DNA.
I also think that my philosophy of treating your brand as a craft
came from the many years I spent watching my dad hone his.

I have a high respect for craftspeople. Two of my business
mentors pursued such work after many successful years in the
business world. Ken Keoughan, my first professional boss in the
advertising industry, studied woodturning after retiring and eventually opened a woodturning school in the mid-coast Maine town
of Damariscotta (*www.woodturningschool.org*). Randy Reynolds,
the former leader of New Business Development at Current, Inc.,
became a luthier specializing in classical guitars (www.reynolds-
guitars.com). Like my dad, both men passed onto me pragmatic

business lessons that I still use today. Both loved the professions they were in before they retired, but love working with their hands even more.

Matthew Crawford's interesting essay in *The New York Times Magazine* entitled "The Case for Working with Your Hands" made me think of my dad and Ken and Randy. Crawford opens with this: "Working in an office, you often find it difficult to see any tangible result from your efforts. What exactly have you accomplished at the end of any given day? Where the chain of cause and effect is opaque and responsibility diffuse, the experience of individual agency can be elusive. *Dilbert, The Office,* and similar portrayals of cubicle life attest to the dark absurdism with which many Americans have come to view their white-collar jobs." I couldn't agree more!

In an unorthodox move, Crawford left his Washington, D.C., think-tank job and opened his own motorcycle repair shop after spending several months with a master mechanic, Fred Cousins of Triple "O" Service. Crawford observed, "As I sat in my K Street office, Fred's life as an independent tradesman gave me an image that I kept coming back to: someone who really knows what he is doing, losing himself in work that is genuinely useful and has a certain integrity to it. He also seemed to be having a lot of fun."

Crawford expands on this essay, his life change and the deeper connection of work/life decisions in his book, *Shop Class as Soulcraft: An Inquiry Into the Value of Work.* I loved this book. It made me think more about what brands might be capable of if brand leaders tended to them as craftspeople tended to their craft. I shared this idea with my two Renaissance-men mentors and they had a lot to say about the matter.

Like my dad, Keoughan is a Type A who demands excellence in all he does. Keoughan confirms that he has always tackled the new vocations and avocations in his life as "crusades." His businesses reflect his personality. Keoughan cares deeply about the work and the people he works with. It is more than business. When he started his own advertising agency in Miami after years of excellent training working on the P&G account in New York, he brought the same discipline, hard work, and strategic planning skills to his own business, but he did it in a Keoughan way, not the typical New York Benton & Bowles big agency way.

Now, in the Woodturning School, he brings that same passion, skill, and intensity to creating a community of like-minded craftspeople. In typical fashion though, Keoughan turned the traditional woodturning school paradigm upside down. "In our school, the woodturning students walk in our doors and are provided with all the tools and the wood and the syllabus they need to find out if this is right for them or not. We have a strategic teaching plan that gets our students immersed in the craft right away. We do not dumb down our program. We have clearly set objectives that are outlined for the students at the start. Our students thank us for this approach. They need and want legitimate feedback. They want direction. They want to learn. They want to be apprenticed."

As a former student of his, I can attest to the fact that Keoughan is an excellent but demanding teacher. His coaching picked up right where my dad's left off. I never wanted to disappoint him in my advertising days. I'm sure his woodturning students don't want to either.

Keoughan believes committees and consensus harm brands. Both often dilute the original vision. "Visions and dreams drive ideas," he said. "Entrepreneurs are not involved with consensus. From Henry Ford to Steve Jobs to Jeff Bezos to the guys at Google—they all were driven, they had a vision, they worked hard to make it happen, their names were on it."

Keoughan uses the term crusade. Randy Reynolds, the luthier, talks about mission and how far our businesses have come from the way work was accomplished back in the days of craft guilds. "Where I think companies and brands go wrong is when the people within those organizations are more career–oriented than mission-oriented. They are spending more time and energy polishing their own careers than crafting the brand to its full potential."

Reynolds, too, understands the power of owning and steering a vision: "My last name is on every classical guitar I make. When I build a custom instrument for someone, I treat it extremely seriously. It's all about the musician. The end user is who counts. I live and breathe the power of that instrument. Everything that I am rides inside that guitar case. When I send out 'The Reynolds,' it is an event for both of us!"

Gary and Susan Lauria, luxury-home builders have this quote as part of their Lauria Builders mission: "Every job is a self-portrait of the person who did it. Autograph your work with excellence." When you run your own company, or turn wooden works of art, or build your own guitars, it is a matter of pride to naturally "autograph your work with excellence." But when you work for a company where you live primarily in the color of your divisional stripe each day and your work is far removed from the actual product, or service, and customer experience that your brand provides, you tend to lose the sense that your work plays an integral role in the overall impact of the brand experience.

Think about your brand. Do the people who work on your brand treat it as a craft or a career? Are there leaders with real vision or committees with consensus? Is there a system of apprenticeship and mentorship in place? Do people seem to love what they do so much that they continually lose themselves in it? Are your brand leaders having fun doing genuinely useful work? How close does your work connect you to your customers? Do your brand leaders see to it that your products or services are 'authographed with excellence' before they go to your customers?

Apprentices and mentors

I have a profound sense of gratitude for my eclectic circle of mentors. These wise guides include people from all walks of life and all ages; and surprisingly, they often mentor me in ways that are outside their fields of expertise. Sometimes their mentorship consists not of words but of actions—how they carry themselves or respond to certain situations. I have simply been an apprentice of their lives. Leadership expert Max De Pree has written quite a bit on this topic. Here's a brief quote from his book, *Mentoring: Two Voices:*

"Mentors guide personal development by formulating questions that trigger responsive thought, that bring the light of experience to the discussion and that encourage breadth rather than narrow focus. Mentors have the opportunity to move the interaction beyond job or career into family matters, other areas of service, areas of study not connected to career. We all ought to know something special—about the arts, about theology or philosophy, about other cultures. One very specific reason to broaden the horizons of our discussions is to remove the fear I have found in many leaders of the creative process and creative people. For organizations that depend on creating change through innovation, such fear is a serious threat. As mentor and mentee move more deeply and intimately into a relationship of real trust and confidence, our personal 'uniquenesses' lead to an expansion of the ground we cover and a comfort with exploring new and unfamiliar territory."

It was said often and factually in the agency and by our clients that 'Freeman will never lie to you or mislead you.' Following his example I've tried to pass on these and other skills I learned from him to those I have worked with."

I also looked outside my industry for advice. Don H. Crist, Ed.D, is a friend who has been running his own consultancy, Effectiveness Associates, for more than 20 years and considers it his mission to create healthy organizations. An expert in conflict resolution and emotional intelligence and a specialist in academic environments, Crist definitely treats his executive coaching practice as a craft. As a faculty member of the prestigious Center for Creative Leadership, I look to Crist as a "master" consultant and consider myself honored to be his unofficial apprentice. In a very informal and humble way, the stories he has shared with me about his own rough spots with clients have helped me tremendously in knowing how to handle some of mine.

Another mentor is a nurse practitioner who has her own private practice. I admire the way she conducts her "business," although she would never use that word. She is the only medical professional I've ever gone to that allows a full hour for office visits. Her integrative, empathetic, unhurried approach allows her patients time for deeper conversation about all areas of their health: emotional, social, biological, psychological, and spiritual. Her caring and holistic manner is reminiscent of "house calls" of a bygone era and of a person deeply committed to her profession. I try to emulate her compassion in the way I do business with my clients.

Perhaps all this talk of personal mentors might encourage you to think about ways your company can better embrace this idea of apprentice-to-journeyman-to-master within your own organizational structure. Or it might spark a conversation about internships, reverse mentoring, or even programs whereby customers are involved in the mentoring process!

Here are a few examples:

Steve Ells is the founder of the innovative fast casual restaurant, Chipotle Mexican Grill. This chain has a position within its company entitled Apprentice. I like that. Here's how it's described on its website:

"As an Apprentice to the General Manager, you will lead your restaurant in successful day-to-day operations. You will continue to train and develop your crew, provide exceptional customer service and maintain budgets set by the General Manager. Under the capable instruction of your General Manager, you will complete a thorough progression through all the duties that will eventually be your secondary and primary responsibilities when you take the next step to becoming General Manager."

Does your brand have a clearly defined learning path?

Other companies ranging in diversity, size, and scope have strong internship programs that are like mini-apprenticeships, a chance for both employee and employer to see if the fit is right. Disney, Build-A-Bear, Google, Microsoft, Compassion International, and Exxon Mobil all have such programs.

Reverse mentoring, the process by which members of the younger digital generation mentor senior executives to help them adapt to changing technology, is another area that brands can participate in to strengthen their overall talent base. Companies like GE and Time Warner have embraced this process. So has public relations firm Edelman. At Edelman, the process is called Rotnem (mentor spelled backwards) and according to the article "Career Advice: Reverse Mentoring Is Revolutionizing the Workplace," about 95 percent of the senior executives in its Chicago office are working with assigned Rotnems. I have some Rotnems in my own life and I appreciate their perspectives and knowledge. I love the ability to see things uniquely through their lens.

In writing *Strengths-Based Leadership,* Rath and Conchie found, "the most effective leaders are always investing in strengths. In the workplace, when an organization's leadership fails to focus on an individual's strengths, the odds of an employee being engaged are a dismal 1 in 11 (9%). But when an organization's leadership focuses on the strengths of its employees, the odds soar to almost 3 in 4 (73%). So that means when leaders focus on and invest in their employees' strengths, the odds of each person being engaged goes up eightfold." Internships, mentoring, and reverse mentoring programs are all about investing not only in an individual's strength, but investing in the long-term strength and power of your brand. Brands need fully engaged, high contributing people who care about the next succession of fully engaged, high contributing people. And wouldn't you like your brand to experience eightfold engagement?

Jeffrey Katzenberg, CEO of DreamWorks Animation SKG, knows what German artist Anton Ehrenzweig meant when he said, "Every student deserves to be treated as a potential genius." In a *Fast Company* interview, Katzenberg describes how brand investment in talent pays off. In acknowledging the contributions of his creative director, Bill Damaschke, he says, "Bill is the student who became better than the teacher. Today, he is much more the creative driver here, and more often than not, I find myself wanting to hear his notes, his critique before my own." Who are your brand students and how are you preparing them to take your role someday?

Sometimes the talk of apprentices and mentors can lead to something even bigger. Harley-Davidson has always done a superb job of making its brand experiential. It is considered one of the top "tattoo brands" that customers feel passionate enough about that they would engrave the company logo on their bodies. In addition to that, Harley-Davidson asked its female customers to go one step further. It asked them to "share their spark," that is, it asked if they would mentor other female riders. They called this their Share Your Spark program. Says Leslie Prevish, market outreach manager, "The mentoring experiences are empowering for both parties involved."

While not so formalized, Keoughan's Woodturning School hosts "Girls Nights Out" where women can tiptoe into this traditional male craft and see if it is something they might enjoy learning. Chocolate truffle cake is complementary when they turn their first wooden bowl!

Is your brand "mentorable" in some way? Have you asked your passionate customers to share their spark with others on your behalf?

Brand barometers

I encourage my clients to look to other brands as mentors to their own. We often discuss brands we lust after and brands we definitely do not want to be like (in this case, a negative rotnem). Naming these two benchmarks is helpful both visually and creatively in crafting our own unique brand voice and experience. For example, when I worked at Current, Inc. one of our brand role models was Hallmark. We admired how well they created meaningful products for "when you care enough to send the very best," and we wanted to find a way to do that for our customers but at a value price and by mail. Having several former Hallmarkers on the staff at Current at the time, we learned that Hallmark lusted after companies like the Metropolitan Museum of Art, Caspari, and Papyrus.

In my own consultancy, I have had the privilege of working with the leaders of Wolferman's, a gourmet English-muffin company, on improving their gift experience. It is no small task to make a simple breakfast food with a well-known inexpensive grocery store competitor "giftable" and worthy of sending as personal or corporate holiday presents. However, we knew other companies did just this with pears, chocolates, oranges, and even popcorn. So we looked to the industry leader, Harry & David, a much larger company with much deeper pockets, for lessons we could emulate. It became our brand mentor. We studied it deeply and tried to master the lessons it offered us as long distance students. I believe we succeeded when eventually Harry & David bought Wolferman's, brought it into its family of brands, and kept intact the strategies we developed.

Brand role models do not even need to be in your own industry and quite often it is better and more liberating when they are not. When I first began my branding work with the folks at Saint Mary's Press, a niche publisher for Catholic teens, we were grasping to find another Christian publisher to emulate. We were just not that wowed by what was happening in the industry. So we looked to other strong brands such as Disney and Apple and spent a great deal of time thinking about curriculum differently than the industry status quo. When we launched the rebranded company, everyone in the industry not only took notice, but also realized this little niche company had big dreams. It went on to become the largest publisher of Catholic teen Bibles.

Thinkering and tinkering

Writers, artists, and musicians bring a sense of craftsmanship to their work naturally. They tinker, they grapple, they dabble, they perfect, they hone, they ponder. I believe this is the work of all brand leaders. Their offices are their ateliers.

Holly Yashi, an artisan-based jewelry company co-founded by

Holly Hosterman and Paul "Yashi" Lubitz, describe their philosophy this way:

> "We believe that beautiful jewelry should gracefully gather a patina of our life experiences. We envision a joyful child discovering her mother's jewelry box, dreaming of the day when she too will wear these treasures, and be warmed by their rich memories.
>
> If a company can have a mission other than simple survival, ours is to resist the current direction the market is taking and suggest another way, where good design isn't something disposable, and you can take pride in something you bought twenty years ago. We believe anything truly valuable takes some care, whether it's your mother's silver or your mother herself. And that the things you wear really can be an expression of who you are; they can make you feel good and brighten the day for others.
>
> We have a story around every piece of jewelry we make, every joint we weld and color we choose. We hand craft each piece right here in our northern California studio. We talk with our artisans every day, eat bagels with them on Friday, and lunch with them the rest of the week. It's a
>
>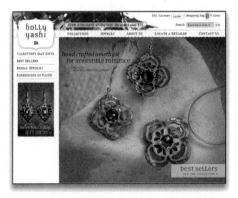
>
> tradition we have here. We might be a little backwards, but we've grown almost every year we've been in business, so maybe there is something to it. It is the only way we would have it. I hope you enjoy this website; it is the culmination of more than 25 years of loving what we do."

As others have mentioned, true craftspeople think of their work as beyond the actual product or service. It is a mission, a crusade, a life philosophy. If your brand were to craft a philosophy, what would it be?

Thos. Moser, designers and builders of fine furniture in Maine, uses the headline "Craftsmanship" in describing what they're all about:

> "As designers and builders of fine furniture we are largely self-taught. If we have teachers, they are the woodworkers of the last century who left a legacy of beautiful forms executed by hand and built to last for generations. Hidden inside our furniture is the stuff of permanence we learned of by taking apart old antiques. Our designs and joinery accommodate for the expansion and contraction of solid wood as the humidity changes."

And, you may not immediately think of Starbucks when you think of the concept of craftsmanship, but that's always the lens founder Howard Schultz has used. He clearly sees Starbucks as a "more than coffee" experience. Starbucks recently ran this ad to remind its customers and potential customers that it does indeed see coffee-making as a craft:

> "We craft our coffees with a passion you can taste. Who knew you'd find true love in the coffee aisle? It's not just coffee. It's Starbucks."

So Moser, Schultz, Hosterman, and Lubitz don't specifically use the word "tinker," but that's indeed what they do with their brands—joyfully, purposefully, proudly.

The Wall Street Journal reported on a bit of tinkering going on inside one of the largest pizza makers in the U.S: "Domino's, founded in 1960, is known for tinkering with its process for making and delivering its pizzas. It claims innovations such as the

'spoodle,' a tool for saucing pizzas, and the corrugated pizza box."
The latest tinkering has "led to a point-of-sale system to woo
customers and streamline online orders where customers can
watch a stimulated photographic version of their pizza as they
select a size, choose a sauce and add pepperoni, black olives and
other toppings. The image changes as ingredients are added or
removed."

I love the word "tinker." Do you remember Tinkertoys, those
simple wooden construction sets in round oatmeal-style contain-
ers? According to the Classic Toy Museum, they were originally
called the "Thousand Wonder Builder" and they were "inspired
by watching children with pencils, sticks, and empty spools of
thread." Someone was thinkering about tinkering when he came
upon this bestseller! And it all came about by paying attention.

How much time does your brand spend tinkering versus dithering? "Dithering" is a state of indecisive agitation and conjures
up the characters in *Dilbert* and *The Office*. Companies can spend
too much time in meetings dithering in silos about things their
customers don't care about and which siphon off time for tinkering
with more important aspects of the brand experience. Increase
your tinkering. Decrease your dithering.

The power of workshopping

I admire two entrepreneurs, Andrea Dupree and Michael Henry,
for their ability to follow their hearts and pursue their dreams.
They moved to Denver fresh from graduating with MFAs from
Emerson College and co-founded Lighthouse Writers Workshop.
As working writers and university-level teachers of writing, their
desire was to launch an independent creative writing program
so that writers could "explore their craft in a supportive yet challenging environment." Non-writers think of the term workshop in

relation to building projects or Santa's toys or perhaps a day-long seminar. Writers use the term workshop as an action verb—as in "let's workshop that chapter." The craft of workshopping is a gentle one.

Dupree says it is also " a constructive one. Writers, who don't normally have a chance to talk to their readers, editors, or others who deem their work as suitable or not suitable for publication, get to sit in on a thorough discussion of their works in progress. A published instructor/mentor guides discussion of the manuscripts, and the group comes up with helpful readings, recommendations, and next steps for the writer to consider. In this way, the writer's own blind spots can be revealed. It's not unusual for one comment to lead to a breakthrough for the writer while she's sitting in the room. Other times, it takes weeks of not thinking about the feedback for some energy for revision to rise up for her. In either case, the workshop process is an attempt to help the writer see his or her own material more objectively and with a freshness that's almost impossible to achieve in isolation."

In workshopping, you refine and recalibrate your original ideas to make them even better. I like to think of brand leaders "workshopping" their brands each and every day, honing them to perfection with, for, and by their customers.

The word 'workshop" is built right into the Build-A-Bear Workshop brand. And craftsmanship is an integral part of its customer experience. The hands-on crafting of a stuffed bear creates an experiential memory that children of all ages will not forget. In case you have never participated in the thrill of taking a young person into one of its stores, this is how it is officially described:

"Guests who visit a Build-A-Bear Workshop enter a recognizable and distinctive teddy bear–themed environment consisting of eight stuffed animal-making stations: Choose Me, Hear Me, Stuff Me, Stitch Me, Fluff Me, Dress Me, Name Me and Take Me Home. Store associates, known

as master Bear Builder associates, share the experience with Guests at each phase of the bear-making process. Regardless of age, Guests enjoy the highly visual environment, the sounds and the fantasy of this special place while they create a memory with their friends and family."

Indeed, it has been a goal of Maxine Clark, Build-A-Bear Workshop founder, chairman and chief executive bear to "put the heart and the fun back into retail." She has succeeded.

Others practice "workshopping their brand" in ways they never thought they might after their first careers. Whether by starting small organic farms selling cheeses, honeys or wines, or by engaging in "encore careers" doing philanthropic work, these entrepreneurs bring their master-level skills and aptitudes from one field into their new journeyman roles. Bill Nelson, president of WineAmerica, a national trade association with more than 800 member wineries, was quoted in *The New York Times* as saying, "Winemaking is a very common second career. Often, people get the financial wherewithal from the first career to get started and transition into wine. Winery owners who have changed careers or added one often find that their varied backgrounds work well in an industry that involves agriculture, chemistry, design, construction and technology. And they are grafting skills they mastered in their previous careers onto the business of turning grapes into wine. That's showing up in winery technology and designs, techniques used to grow grapes, locations that break with tradition and, most of all, a greater emphasis on business plans, spreadsheets and new marketing approaches."

Again, the philosophy and soul of craftsmanship can be brought into any brand experience, from English muffins to stuffed bears to jewelry, furniture, writing programs, and vineyards.

Is it time for a little bit of workshopping for your brand?

The necessary MBA: Master of Being Attentive

I agreed with what Sir Isaac Newton had to say: "If I have ever made any valuable discoveries, it has been owing more to patient attention than to any other talent." I've already shared examples of lessons that brand-builders could learn from craftspeople. But here's another important observation from Crawford, our wise motorcycle repairman, "There is an ethic of paying attention that develops in the trades through hard experience. Getting it right demands that you be *attentive* in the way of a conversation rather than in the way of a demonstration. I believe the mechanical arts have a special significance for our time because they cultivate not creativity, but the less glamorous virtue of attentiveness. Things need fixing and tending no less than creating."

I call this a real life MBA. That is, earning a masters in being attentive. We are the antithesis of an attentive society. Yes, we perform "due diligence" when we are looking into new ventures or new businesses, but do we apply that same vigilance to our existing brands? It seems to me that our brands suffer from the same attention deficit disorder of our business lives—the hurrying, the text messaging, the catch-you-in-the-hallway handoff, the quick hire, the turning over of this piece of the brand experience to that department, etc. Yes we may agree that our brands need fixing and tending, but who will apply the thoughtfulness to these tasks? Who are the master craftspeople of your brand? And are they training any apprentices?

The art of making fine furniture requires close attention. The folks at Thos. Moser specialize in this. Here's the story of their Customer In Residence program in their own words:

> "It all started when we had a long-standing customer ask if he could spend his vacation 'interning' in our shop and learning how to make something special with his own two hands. It was an unusual request, but we said 'why not' and set him up with a cabinetmaker from the shop and let them work side-by-side for about a week or so. It was such a great experience that he encouraged us to develop it into a program so we could offer the opportunity to others. This program has become very important to the company for several reasons: The first and foremost of which is creating a deeper connection between us and our customers by creating an experience that cannot be duplicated. Based on the feedback of the first groups, we seem to have achieved this goal. This program also allows us to get closer to our roots as woodworkers by sharing the nuances of a craft that could otherwise be lost if not passed along. And of course there is the 'halo effect' that will come from the participants themselves after they leave our shop and share their experiences with their friends, families and colleagues."

Scott Wentzell, marketing manager at Thos. Moser Cabinetmakers, tells us more: "Brand is not just a logo or a tagline or even a product, it is the core essence of what makes a company successful. It has to be real, not only to customers but to employees as well. Our Customer In Residence program, which brings some of our best customers into the shop to build a piece of furniture alongside our craftsmen, helped us to realize this. When a customer spends a week inside our company working side-by-side with our employees and leaves feeling even more passionate about what we do and reiterating our brand attributes back to us without any coaching, then we know that our brand is more than just a marketing campaign."

Living with your customers for week-long intervals? Working side-by-side? Listening, paying attention, learning, tinkering, workshopping. Can you think of a more compelling way for brands to spend their time? That is indeed soulcraft!

Craft Your Brand Homework

⫸ The lists

Who mentored you? Make a list. The Harvard Mentoring Project started a "Thank Your Mentor Day" a few years ago to help bring visibility to this important topic. Whether you decide to participate in this formal national program or find a creative way to do so informally, do thank your mentors. Perhaps one of the most meaningful ways to show gratitude is to mentor another. Like Davies requested of his direct reports at Standard Chartered, make a list of the people who might need, want, or desire a mentor both in and outside your brand. It doesn't have to be formal. Just hang out with them. Have a cup of tea or coffee or microbrew. Listen. Pay attention. Learn. Pay it forward. Max De Pree reminds us: "Mentoring is above all a work of love, which at its best is a two-way exchange."

⫸ Face time

If you read *Soulcraft,* you'll discover that there are many reasons Crawford finds more fulfillment in his work as a motorcycle repairman than his former, supposedly more pres-tigious job at the Washington think tank. For one, "The core experience is one of individual responsibility, supported by face-to-face interactions between tradesman and customer." Ask your five top brand leaders to reflect back on their past year of brand accomplishments. How many were the result of direct face-to-face interactions with their customers? What do you think might have been accomplished if these leaders spent more time that way? Start a conversation about how you and your leaders can spend more time face-to-face (or, even better, side-by-side like Thos. Moser). How can you assure that next year will be different?

⨂ Two powerful letters

Tinkering takes time. The word "tinker" contains two of the same lowly one-point Scrabble letters as are in "dither"—E and R, but tinkering is much more productive than dithering. Tinkering requires hands-on action and involvement. Why not have your brand team play with those two letters and create as many word possibilities as you can imagine. Here's a start:

Re	Er
Reimagine	Simpler
Recalibrate	Easier
Rebrand	Smarter
Reenergize	Better
Reignite	Stronger
Retool	Cheaper
Reinvent	Smaller
Rejuvenate	Faster

Then, write your top 12 **RE** and **ER** favorite words on separate index cards. Pass out one card per team member and have them write three ways your brand could reimagine, recalibrate, or rebrand itself or become smarter, better, stronger. Now, take some thinkering time to mull over your tinkering and see what happens next! See which brand leaders want to sign up for putting their "autograph of excellence" on some of these key initiatives.

⫷ Think with your hands

In a *Fast Company* interview, Perry Kleban, CEO of Timbuk2, said his favorite life lesson from IDEO's David Kelley was to: "Think with your hands, build something or try something, then talk about it, not the reverse." What branding issue is top of mind for you right now? Try following Kelley's advice and see what happens.

8

Reveal Your Branners Winsomeness

WHY DO I FEEL that many companies just don't care about my business? I am incredulous about the *hauteur* of companies these days. They act as if they don't need customers. With hardly a thank you at checkout, with policies that place barriers to doing business with them in my way, and with the lack of information and helpfulness in the purchasing channel I am physically in, I wonder what happened to brand manners. Branners for short.

Perhaps this lack of attentiveness and appreciation is simply a reflection of our times. Comedian Jerry Seinfeld riffed about our constant barrage of incivilities, "We've fallen into a trap of ever-widening orbits of contact (BlackBerries, cell phones) and there is a total disregard for the present moment." Brands are not immune. I have experienced too much "total disregard for the present customer experience moment" and I'm certain you have too. Chatting with friends brings out story after story of customer experiences that are time-consuming, rude, illogical, and ungracious. We are tired of being treated as if our business doesn't matter.

Perhaps it's time for companies to pay a bit more attention to their branners and examine all their brand touchpoints with a higher goal than just completing civil transactions. Brands that want to win their customers' hearts should strive for winsomeness. Maybe we need a new acronym to give this practice more caché, perhaps BWEs—Branner Winsomeness Evaluations. Maybe they should occur often.

And maybe we need attention from the very top. Max De Pree, former CEO of furniture maker Herman Miller, Inc., said, "The first responsibility of a leader is to define reality. The last is to say thank you. In between, the leader is the servant." Ann McGee-Cooper and Duane Trammell agree and write that servant leadership "is not about a personal quest for power, prestige, or material rewards. Instead, from this perspective, leadership begins with a true motivation to serve others." Do you, as a brand leader, have a servant's heart?

What have you done lately to serve your customers?

I usually immerse myself in my clients' brand experiences when I begin to work with them. I anonymously place orders in their various channels and I pay close attention to how I am treated. I also monitor their competitors and do the same with each of them. I bring all this customer experience feedback to my clients, playing back actual phone orders for them to hear, showing them the condition that their products arrive in, and demonstrating the internal and external packaging as a customer might. Every time I do this, the clients are surprised by some aspect of the experience that is just not up to the standards it thought it had in place. It is a humbling moment. Problems get uncovered, policies get questioned, fierce conversations take place, and enhancements to the customer experience are made. The BWE meter gains some attention and next time, hopefully, the customer will benefit from being served a better brand experience.

Excellent branners are a vitally important brand differentiation tool. Companies that have a servant's heart, that purposefully treat their customers as friends, that hone the present customer moment, that practice something beyond common civility, that show genuine appreciation towards their customers, and that have a sense of joy in all they do will attract more loyalty. These acts of winsomeness are what set good brands apart from great brands.

Southwest Airlines makes excellent branners just a natural part of the way it does business. It outlines its corporate culture this way on its website:

- Servant's heart
- Follow the golden rule
- Adhere to the basic principles
- Treat others with respect
- Put others first
- Be egalitarian
- Demonstrate proactive customer service
- Embrace the SWA family

First and foremost on this list is a servant's heart. "Serving" is not a word our culture uses much these days. How well does your brand help your customers accomplish their goals? Does your brand make your customers smile?

Befriend your customers

When they speak about their customers, I encourage companies not to use terms like target audiences, end users, consumers, wallets, eyeballs or giving units. These are extremely impersonal business words and can create misperceptions about behavior that brand leaders expect from their customers versus what they, as real, live, busy, multitasking people like you and me might actually do. It is better for brands to think of their customers as friends.

Brands that befriend their customers "get" them and show true compassion to their needs. Brands that befriend their customers know what bugs them. They also know what their dreams are. Brands that befriend their customers act as advocates on their behalf.

Marketing professor Kyle Murray, writing in the *Financial Post,* said, "My research suggests that retailers are going to have to become better advocates for their customers. The big box stores with enormous selections will need to help people make choices. They will have to continue to simplify store navigation and take advantage of emerging technologies that improve the shopping experience. This will likely include the mass customization of products and services, without adding to consumers' decision-making burden."

For Donna Sheloski, the owner of three Curves fitness clubs, advocating for her customers and treating them as friends just comes naturally. It's also part of Curves' business model. Sheloski told me: "The founder of Curves often reminds franchisees that our business is very simple: Getting members and keeping members. The brand is what draws them in, with its history of helping women meet their health and fitness goals. Women continue coming, however, not only because of their results, but because they've developed deep friendships with other members and the Curves staff. From day one we make a point of not only memorizing every woman's name, but befriending them as well. I tell my staff, 'Imagine each woman wears a sign that says MMFS, that is, Make Me Feel Special.'"

Alicia Ann Mangham, senior account director for AstraZeneca Pharmaceuticals knows that befriending customers means making them feel special no matter what their current position, their immediate project, or their present company. With 15 years of experience at AstraZeneca calling on medical directors and vice presidents of pharmacies, Mangham has seen her customers through many industry changes. "My pharmaceutical customers tend to switch companies every 2 to 3 years. My success has been very dependent on developing relationships that were not project specific or organizationally dependent. When I moved past relationships built only on immediate needs and outcomes and into deeper personal relationships, I realized I had gained customers for life. More importantly, it made my work more fun and personally rewarding!"

How well does your brand champion your customers' needs? Do you make life easier or harder for them? How do you make them feel special?

Try this exercise: Take a moment and make two lists. On one list, write down three things that bug you. Anything. On the other list, write down three things that you know bug your best friend. Here's a few to get you started:

- Coupons that have expired by the time you get to use them

- Scratchy tags inside clothing

- Sitting at a desk

- Loving flannel sheets in the winter but being married to someone who doesn't

- Wanting to stay in shape but having limited time to pursue this goal

What does this have to do with branner winsomeness? Well, brands that befriend their customers go out of their way to please their customers. And in order to know how to please them, they have to know enough about what bugs them and what delights them. They know what ticks them off and what tickles them. Like dear friends, great brands try to solve problems for their friends and do more of the things that bring their customers joy and fewer of the things that irritate them. It's that simple.

Let's look at the following examples for ways that brands understand that the personal is indeed universal, that thinking about your customers as friends with problems you can solve just makes good sense.

When you hear the name Bed Bath & Beyond, you immediately see those bright blue 20 percent off coupons that have become its trademark promotional tactic. It distributes those oversized coupons by email, postal mail, and nationwide advertising circulars. It runs full-page ads with those same coupons. The coupons seem to be everywhere. Bed Bath & Beyond brand leaders know that buying items like towels, linens, and pots and pans from the retailer is not the same as your weekly run for bread, milk, and lunch meat. You may not have a need for one of its products for months. That's okay. As a befriending brand, it understands that when you are ready to buy, it wants to be ready to save you money. You can use one of its blue 20 percent off coupons *anytime,* even if they are expired. Bed Bath & Beyond rewards your shopping behavior at your convenience. This delights its customers. More retailers should adopt this tactic.

Friends often chat about the little things in life. Years ago, Hanes listened to its customers grumbling about the nuisance of scratchy tags in their underwear. As a brand that befriends its customers, it not only listened, it did something about it. Hanes created tag-free tee-shirts. Poking fun at the whole irritating concept, it launched a "gotagless.com" website and hosted "retirement parties" for the tags where it provided humorous suggestions for what to do with all the "retired" tags: "throw at bride and groom," use as "placemats for Barbie dolls," or as "luggage tags for people named Hanes." Tackling this seemingly minor annoyance brought it brand loyalty and made its customers smile. Note that several other companies, including Lands' End have now gone tagless.

In the third grade I had a hard time sitting at my desk all day long. It seemed so confining; I needed to move about. Now, more than three decades later, long periods of desk time have gotten worse. I know I am not alone in this. Some people sit on balance balls at their desks to relieve back pain and pressure; others give up sitting altogether and stand to do their work. The Stand-Up Desk Company was started by a man whose back ached from sitting too long at his desk. Now there are complex Walkstation Desks and TrekDesks that combine treadmill walking with your desk work. These brands have all befriended their customers by doing more than just walking a mile in their shoes; they literally redesigned the ride for them to make it both more comfortable and productive. Brands that befriend their customers focus on outcomes.

Some single product brands befriend their customers by solving problems customers have completely given up on. David W. Haggerty faced a marital predicament shared by many: his wife loved the warmth of flannel sheets, but he did not. He took on the challenge of marital bliss and created Split the Sheets, a set of fitted and flat sheets and pillowcases split with polar fleece on one side and cotton on the other. Needless to say, he found a larger captive audience. My mother-in-law, truly a wise woman, sent us these ingenious half-flannel and half-cotton sheets one year for Christmas. Everyone I tell about these sheets agrees that the world needs products like these! Brands that befriend their customers know that the personal is universal.

Then there's the FitFlop Footwear company based in London. With over four million pairs of shoes sold in the first two years of doing business, FitFlop befriended its customers by helping them do double duty: get a workout while walking. Its goal simply stated is to "make it easier for people to stay in shape." According to its website, its patented "microwobbleboard technology helps its customers increase leg, calf, and gluteal muscle activity, improving posture and muscle tone." FitFlop Footwear knows what its customers "wouldn't dream of living without."

Now, take a look at your two lists. What did you discover from your examples? How well does your brand "get" your customers? Are there any "personal yet universal" intimacies that apply to your brand?

Show compassion

Brands befriend their customers by showing compassion in big and not-so-big ways.

It is quite apparent that the world does not revolve around left-handed people or tea drinkers. I am amazed at how many fine restaurants and hotels show total disregard for the tea drinker all the while going overboard to accommodate the coffee drinker. I have found it nearly impossible to find a cup of high-quality decaf black tea to accompany my dessert in the evening. I have resorted to bringing my own tea bags with me and simply asking for a cup of hot water. Luckily, the folks at Republic of Tea empathize with this tea drinker's dilemma and created the perfect creative solution for just these situations. Their Traveler's Tea tins are small and compact and fit in almost any evening bag or briefcase. They easily hold six round teabags and are refillable. The "Ministers of Sipware" at Republic of Tea have thought through their customers' needs in every aspect of the tea experience and are poised to accommodate those needs. They clearly state that they are "committed to taking care of our customers in a kind, respectful, and compassionate way and to building long-term, mutually rewarding relationships with our suppliers, customers, communities, and each other." Brands that befriend their customers present compassionate solutions.

Most women have a love-hate relationship with pantyhose. Sara Blakely was no exception. Founder of the beloved shapewear company Spanx, Blakely befriended women across the country when she invented a whole new category of undergarments by cutting out the feet of her pantyhose in order to look better in her off-white pants and open toe sandals many years ago. "I never dreamed visible panty lines and uncomfortable thongs would inspire me to become an inventor," she said. This female entrepreneur turned an everyday problem into a $300 million business venture simply by having compassion first for herself, then for women everywhere. Blakely continues to listen to her customers' gripes and present ever more empathetic solutions to their problems. Her newest invention, the Bra-llelujah, was designed to eliminate back fat and visible bra lines. Spanx specializes in compassion.

So does Rhonda Brennan, broker/owner of Mountain Desert Realty. She not only befriends her customers as she works to find them their next home or sell their existing home, she celebrates with them in an "above and beyond" way upon closing. She knows firsthand what a stressful time this is for her clients, so she compassionately jumps in and extends her services. Brennan shared this with me: "One of the great things I offer each of my clients is a house warming party after closing. I do it all: prepare and mail invitations, even catering and hosting the party. It is a huge success. My clients love 'showing off' their new home and having their family and friends share the celebration with them. I take photos during the party and share them with my clients and their guests (when I send them a thank you for attending and helping my client celebrate such a wonderful occasion). I get rave reviews each and every time I do this. It is so much fun for everyone—and a great way to create new relationships for my business!".

Sherwin Williams is another company that "gets" its customers' needs. While its goal is to sell paint, and hopefully lots of it, it really only wants to sell customers the exact color that will delight them. It knows this is best accomplished through trial and error and Sherwin Williams' branding strategy is to be a low-risk, compassionate partner in that process. With Color-To-Go paint samples, customers can buy small amounts for test painting. Its Color Visualizer allows customers to upload their own home images and try various paint colors on the screen. By befriending its customers in all the various paint decision pain points, Sherwin Williams differentiates itself among its competitors.

As a parent, Ann Ruethling, co-founder of children's book company, Chinaberry, was "disturbed by the lack of caring and respect expressed in many of the children's books she found at the library for her daughter Elizabeth." She then set out to find positive and uplifting books. This is how she explains what happened next: "Much work went into that little project of mine. I subscribed to numerous children's literature publications and scouted out as many libraries as I could. I started keeping notes on index cards about the books I liked and at what age I wanted to introduce Elizabeth to each book. By the time my stack of index cards was three or four inches high, I began to realize how much time and energy had gone into this mission of mine. And I realized there were probably a lot of other concerned parents who could greatly benefit from my stack of 3x5's. I felt that if parents could just feed all those wonderful books into the hearts and minds of their children, the world would have to become a better place. Thus, Chinaberry was conceived—at first as a free service, and then as a catalog business to make it easier for parents to buy the books I was telling them about."

Nearly 30 years later, Chinaberry continues to show compassion for children, for other busy parents, and for its desire to make the whole world a better place through its offerings in its two collections, Chinaberry and Isabella. Ruethling remains a discerning merchant: "Both of our catalogs strive to truly enrich the lives of those who order from them. We are not about cluttering people's lives with yet more stuff. My merchandising staff uses, tests, researches, reads, wears whatever it is that she has decided has a chance of making it into the catalogs. It's not an exaggeration to say that for every one product that is in the catalogs, we've considered and discussed 99 others. We don't want to offer for sale anything that we wouldn't have in our own lives. It's true that both Chinaberry and Isabella were founded as an answer to a need we had as parents and as adults, and that fact helps to continue to guide us to make the right choices for us, and to educate our customers about our products."

Despite its carefree tagline, Nike knows there is nothing easy for its customers when it comes to "just doing it." Nike knows that having goals and supportive friends makes "just doing it" even more doable. By creating Nike Plus, a running community, and SportBand, a device to track runs, this brand lends its supportive services as a complement to its running shoes. Perhaps that is why *Brandweek* declared Nike Plus the digital campaign of the decade. "Nike Plus takes "Just Do It" and actually helps runners get it done. Nike Plus is credited with powering Nike's gains in the running shoe category." According to the company, NikePlus.com now has two million members who have tallied over 100 million miles. Nike is just showing compassion for its customers' dreams.

Electronics category leader Best Buy is a befriending brand that shows compassion in a different way. It knows that every time it sells a new device, the customer probably has one she'll need to get rid of. Best Buy wants to make every aspect of the buying, selling and tossing process easy. CEO Brian Dunn had this to say in *Fortune:* "We're transitioning from being just a mover of boxes. We want to help customers get better use of technology, whether they are buying, installing, fixing, or disposing of their hardware." Here's how it advertises on its website:

> "You trust us when it's time to buy the latest electronics. You can also trust us to help you safely dispose of your old ones. In fact, many of your broken, obsolete, or unwanted gadgets are just waiting to be reincarnated. So bring them to us. And we'll make sure they're properly and safely recycled, so they have the chance to perhaps come back as something even cooler in the future. It's all part of our Greener Together™ program. And we'll take just about anything electronic, including TVs, DVD players, computer monitors, cell phones and more. You can bring in up to two items a day, per household, and most things are absolutely free. So do it for the Earth. Do it to get rid of some old junk. Or just do it for some good Karma."

Best Buy's empathy for the practical post-purchase aspects that its customers have to deal with wins it support. In an interview with Best Buy's CMO, Barry Judge, *Brandweek* reported, "The concept of Customer Service 3.0 is to go where the conversation is happening. Our people can help before, during, and after the sale. We're a chain of a lot of people who are dedicated to that mission. Our strategy is to communicate that our people are the difference. We're accessible. You can reach us through the web, store social media, and we'd like to help before and after the sales." Brands that befriend their customers know that compassion is a round-the-clock job.

Better than ever

In its 8th Annual Merchant Survey, The E-Tailing Group found that offering exemplary customer service was the number one way to retain its online customers. I believe that practice holds true in any channel. President Lauren Freedman told me, "It is one of the last true differentiators in a world where price and product have become commoditized and fads come and go. Going the extra mile for your customers will never go out of style." *BusinessWeek* featured a cover story on the topic of Extreme Customer Service and highlighted the fact that even in this tight economy, the "winners in their annual ranking of Customer Service Champs are treating their best customers better than ever."

This is a philosophy that guided P&G's CEO A.G. Lafley. *Forbes* reported, "When Lafley took over P&G in 2000, his leadership actions quickly breathed life into a stagnating company. He placed a premium on putting the customer first. He not only defined two pivotal moments of truth for consumers, the moment of the decision to buy and that of delight in use; he also demonstrated ways to make those moments of truth ever more truthful. He regularly observed customers in their homes and in the marketplace to see first-hand how well P&G delivered on those two moments of truth." Have you examined your moments of truth to see how they can be "ever more truthful"?

Here's what happens if you go to Zappos.com:

> "Customer Service Is Everything. In Fact, It's The Entire Company. We've been asked by a lot of people how we've grown so quickly, and the answer is actually really simple. We've aligned the entire organization around one mission: to provide the best customer service possible. Internally, we call this our WOW philosophy."

CEO Tony Hsieh sees himself as part of the customer service. In December, during one of the company's busiest times ever, he tweeted: "Spending the afternoon taking phone calls from customers! If you call Zappos today, you might get me :) "

Winsome brands that hone the present and future customer moments indeed work hard to make them "ever more truthful."

Laura Brady, former Three Dog Bakery VP & general manager of franchise bakery operations and e-commerce told me, "At Three Dog Bakery one of our guiding brand principles was that 'we loved dogs and dogs loved us.' It was on every one of our packages and was the reason we used premium ingredients in our all-natural baked food and treats. We wouldn't feed our own dogs anything less than the best. But our love didn't stop there. The Three Dog Bakery brand focused on strengthening the relationship between humans and their dogs. Whether offering a taste of all-natural carrot cake to each dog that came to our bakeries or throwing a 'growloween' costume contest for dogs and humans, we wanted each dog to salivate for more Three Dog Bakery treats and each human to smile watching his/her dog enjoy our products. We knew most dogs were not discriminating eaters, but most humans chose treats that made them smile on the inside knowing they did something good for their dog." Like the folks at Best Buy, the brand leaders at Three Dog Bakery understood just how valuable brand smiles are during and after the sale.

Eileen Spitalny, founder of Fairytale Brownies along with her partner David Kravetz, has built a brand that revolves around "supreme customer service." Spitalny and Kravetz hone all aspects of the customer experience. Spitalny shared this with me: "When we started Fairytale Brownies our goal was not only to always make the best brownie but also to have the best customer service, shipping experience, and creative and custom packaging. From the beginning we wanted our customers to know every contact with us would be supreme. So we had to act like the big guys even when we were the little guys. We knew we wanted to create a brand so when you saw our logo with the little guy with the spoon, you knew it was Fairytale—you see purple and brown, then it must be Fairytale; colorful banded chocolate brown boxes, it's Fairytale; get a fax or an email from us, it's Fairytale.

"In building our Fairytale brand we have always been keenly aware that each touch point with customers, vendors, and employees conveys our brand message and promise. Our customer guarantee is called 'Our Pure Promise' and our tagline is 'A Taste of Pure Enchantment.' Baking all natural, top quality brownies with incomparable customer service and innovative custom packaging is our true and authentic 'pure' promise and taste that we speak of in these messages. Our catalog and website conveys this with photography and the language we use in the copy. Our facility and employees emulate this through our uniform policy, building materials, colors, and voice mail and email signatures that end with 'Have a Fairytale Day!' We strive to communicate pure, authenticity, premium, enchanting yet mature. We strive to communicate we are uncompromising in everything we do."

How does your brand perfect every aspect of customer service? Are you satisfied that it is "ever more truthful"? Would you say that it is supreme? That it will make your customers smile?

Show genuine appreciation

I am grateful that I grew up with a manners-conscious mom. My sisters and I joke that she wanted us to write thank you notes practically as the gifts were being unwrapped. Despite our childhood protestations at the time, expressing gratitude is a habit that serves me well. I am especially attentive to this habit or lack of it in the business world. Companies spend a lot of time and money to say "Can we please have your business?" Befriending brands go the next step and take the time to say thank you after the customers give them their business.

These expressions of gratitude take many forms. Here's a branded note card that came tucked inside my last order from women's fashion apparel company, Boston Proper:

Thank You!

We hope you love your Boston Proper fashions. Much thought & effort has gone into ensuring their distinctive design and quality, with just the right amount of sexy. You inspire us & we thank you for wearing it like no one else.

Sheryl Clark
President

P.S. Free shipping on your next order. Details in the enclosed catalog.

6500 Park of Commerce Boulevard, Boca Raton, Florida 33487 • 1-800-411-4080 • bostonproper.com

I like this for many reasons: it's short and sweet; it's from the president; it reinforces the brand; it tells me that I, the customer, inspire their company; it rewards me in the future. It makes me smile. This simple, five-sentence correspondence shows me that Boston Proper treats its customers as friends. As American statesman Henry Clay said, "Courtesies of a small and trivial character are the ones which strike deepest in the grateful and appreciating heart."

Brand courtesy is really what branners winsomeness is all about. Brands of all sizes can practice it and this is one case where smaller brands often do have the advantage over bigger companies. Think about your favorite neighborhood independent restaurant or bakery or coffee shop or flower shop. You probably know the owners and they know you. You appreciate doing business with them and they, too, appreciate the business you bring them. Dean and I frequent a lovely little Italian bistro in the foothills of the Rocky Mountains called Bella Panini. We are always greeted by name and our friends are treated like special guests. The Trombley husband and wife team run the restaurant as if they have just opened their home to friends. They don't use words like 'servant leadership' but that's just the attitude they model and instill in all their staff. K.T. Trombley shared this with me, "In the highly competitive restaurant business, it is not enough just to have a good concept, good food, or both. You want people to take ownership in what you do. Both the employees and the customers. It brings me great joy to see our customers bring their friends and family in around the holidays and describe Bella as 'their place.' That's what Pat and I strive for—to make our customers feel like part of our family."

I appreciate that Talbot's, Bliss Spa, and Aveda all send me a birthday card each July with some type of practical reward no matter how much business I've done with them that year. And, as frequent flier, I also appreciate that Frontier Airlines ran the ad at left on *its* birthday thanking all its customers.

The Wall Street Journal reported on this brand thank you from Alaska Airlines: "After boarding, Alaska Airlines flight attendants deliver their favorite drinks to elite-level customers when they are sitting in coach, thanking them by name for their business. 'The point is not the cocktail. The point is the recognition and thanks for your business,' said Steve Jarvis, vice president of sales and customer experience for Alaska, a unit of Alaska Air Group, Inc." I once experienced something similar on Frontier Airlines when the flight attendant thanked me by name for returning as a frequent flyer. Ever since that one time, I have wondered why this does not happen more often.

Other companies use more than notes and words and small gestures to express gratitude to their customers. They make it an event and add a dose of humor. For the last several years, quick service restaurant Chick-fil-A offers a free meal to any customer who visits one of its restaurants fully dressed as a cow. In a recent press release, Steve Robinson, Chick-fil-A's senior vice president of marketing said: "Cow Appreciation Day continues to be one of our best indicators of the great passion our customers have for the brand. It takes a loyal fan to dress like a cow for a free meal. Based on the stories we hear from our restaurant opera-

tors around the country, we have quite a large—and growing—base of Chick-fil-A fans. Cow Appreciation Day is our way of thanking them for their loyalty, not to mention a truly fun day!"

It's not just customers who notice good branners. Other companies do too. Listen to what Phil Minix, president of MCM Electronics says: "MCM Electronics has several competitors within each product category we sell. In addition, we have competition within industry segments. Because we are distributors of other manufacturer's goods, many of which have MAPP (Minimum Advertised Pricing Policies) and authorized service center pricing, we have to find ways to differentiate our-selves from competitors who are selling the same products. We have chosen to do this with the customer experience. In general, we have better return policies, offer free technical support and try to provide more information on our website than competitors. We are also in development of an improved experience in our call center. We want to 'WOW!' our customers with our choice of words and by thanking them for their past business. We were inspired with this from our local Chick-fil-A and their outstanding customer service . . . how they say 'My Pleasure' after you say 'Thank You,' etc. It's a very simple thing but we believe has a big impact.

"So we are developing a language that we want to use on the phones and also the systems to support our ability to thank cus-tomers for their past business. If you are an existing customer and call into our call center, we will be able to quickly see on screen how many times you've purchased, how much you've spent, and what your last transaction was. This way we will be able to say 'Hello Mr. Smith, thanks for calling again, I see you're one of our most loyal customers and want to thank you for your past business. I also see you made a return a couple of weeks ago and just wanted to make sure we handled everything OK for you? OK, great. So how may I help you today?'

"We expect this specific gratitude to help us further reinforce our thanks for our customers' loyalty and encourage them to think of us every time they need the kinds of products we sell."

Here's another example of excellent brand manners. Near the end of 2009, Levenger's Steve Leveen posted this on his blog:

The CEO says thanks

It's been a year, hasn't it?

To all of you who have been part of the Levenger community this year, I thank you. From the start, we've been a company that knows the value and rewards of conversing with our customers. Who better to tell us whether we're doing a good job?

If 2009 was good for anything, it was to remind us of what is truly important and what can never be lost, taken away, canceled, downgraded, or eliminated. Our ability to read ignites our capacity to think and stirs our desire to do—to do the good, important work that each one of you does for your community and your family and yourself.

Here's to more of such good work in 2010—to a life well-lived through reading.

Here's to you.

With gratitude,

Steve

French author Pierre Marivaux reminds us that "in this world, you must be a bit too kind in order to be kind enough." First, does your brand express its gratitude to your customers? And second, is this expression too kind or simply kind enough? Like you, I love doing business with companies that are too kind!

Playful attitude

Friends enjoy one another's company. They have fun being together. Brands are no different. Today, many brands have a sense of frolicsomeness and humor as part of their brand charter no matter what their product or service. It's simply part of what makes them winsome. Management consultant Tom Peters lists fun and playfulness as one of his "entrepreneurial excellence ten must haves."

In addition to its servant's heart attitude, Southwest Airlines prides itself on its "Fun-LUVing Attitude:

- Have Fun
- Don't take yourself too seriously
- Maintain perspective (balance)
- Celebrate successes
- Enjoy your work
- Be a passionate team player

In addition to its quirky and entertaining flight attendants, Southwest does little, inexpensive things like offer its customers downloadable "Mommy Patches," stickers that say "My Peanut and I fly Southwest." It befriends its mom customers and tries to make flying fun

for travelers who are juggling babies, car seats, and diaper bags. Frontier accomplishes this in its own cheeky way by painting

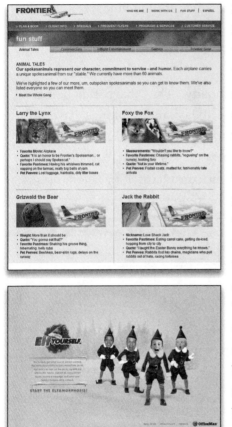

its planes with 60 unique animals. From Grizwald the Bear to Flip the Bottle-Nosed Dolphin to Larry the Lynx, the company says, "our spokesanimals represent our character, commitment to service and humor."

OfficeMax started its jocular "Elf Yourself" free holiday e-greeting in 2006 and it has become "the most popular viral experience in web history." According to Bob Thacker, SVP of marketing and advertising for OfficeMax, "Elf Yourself has become a holiday tradition—part of popular culture. In fact, according to a brand study we have conducted, 95 percent of people who have been 'elfed' in the past requested that we bring it back for this holiday season. We look forward to once again giving consumers a cost-effective way to celebrate the season and bring back the holiday spirit at a time when it's needed most." In 2009, Hip Hop Elves and Singing Elves joined past favorites (Disco Elves and Country Elves) and the original Classic Elves as customers had a bit of brand fun "elfing" friends and family and coworkers.

Zappos is bold about making fun part of its culture and headlines one of its corporate tabs with this: "We're Always Creating Fun and A Little Weirdness!" It explains further:

"One of the things that makes Zappos different from a lot of other companies is that we value being fun and being a little weird. We don't want to become one of those big companies that feels corporate and boring. We want to be able to laugh at ourselves. We look for both fun and humor in our daily work. This means that many things we do might be a little unconventional—or else it wouldn't be a little weird. We're not looking for crazy or extreme weirdness though. We want just a touch of weirdness to make life more interesting and fun for everyone. We want the company to have a unique and memorable personality. One of the side effects of encouraging weirdness is that it encourages people to think outside the box and be more innovative. When you combine a little weirdness with making sure everyone is also having fun at work, it ends up being a win-win for everyone: Employees are more engaged in the work that they do, and the company as a whole becomes more innovative."

An article in *Business Week* reported that in addition to the shoe and service business, Zappos is now sharing its branners practices with other like-minded companies.

Bliss Spa makes fun part of its employee application screening process (and note its low tolerance reference to silo-behavior):

"A sense of humor is a 'plus', along with a scrupulous work ethic, resolute disdain of 'slackers', possibly 'unhealthy' love for all things related to grooming, and a good soul. (No interoffice politics are indulged here . . . we have too much to accomplish.) We are a serious spa/skincare company with a witty edge, so you must have the personality to match. The ability to slough off stress and maintain an upbeat attitude is crucial to success . . . for those looking to glow with us!"

Republic of Tea looks for similar fun-loving employees but its charter states it in a slightly different way: "Our purpose is to enrich people's lives through the experience of fine tea and the

Sip by Sip rather than Gulp by Gulp lifestyle—a life of health, balance and well-being. We value patience, persistence, initiative, resourcefulness, courage and a good sense of humor. We appreciate beauty, simplicity and genuine content."

Many companies are doing their best to associate their brands with positivity. Ice cream company Cold Stone Creamery simply says, "We will make people happy." Sportswear brand Fresh Produce wants both its customers and employees to "Live the FP life! We hope wearing Fresh Produce will inspire you to shine, be your best and do a little good even if it simply means adding a smile to your daily agenda to make someone's day brighter."

In today's trying economy, Kodak wants to befriend its customers by taking smiling to the next level. It launched an "It's Time to Smile" integrated marketing campaign as a follow-up to its Brightside Tour with The Compliment Guys (two Purdue university students sharing adulations around the countryside). The new Kodak Smile Meter and Kodak Smile Maker social media applications are designed to "make it easier and more fun to share smiles and photos."

Brands that take frolicking seriously befriend their customers by becoming memorable for an attitude that says, we want to add joy to your lives. Does your brand add or subtract joy for your customers? What can you do to take your joy factor to the next level?

Reveal Your Branners Winsomeness Homework

》 Mother was right

Manners really are important. How are your brand manners? Winsome or *wince*some? Conduct your own fierce BWE

(Branners' Winsomeness Evaluation) report card and start to shore up those C+ (or less) areas. Brands that befriend their customers go for straight A's. Make winsomeness more than a brand evaluation project; make it a way of doing business each and every day.

⫸ A "go all in" gratitude fest

I liked what innovative marketer Seth Godin had to say on his blog: "If you're going to do something, do it. Go all in. Doing it half in makes no sense at all to me. It's like a store that has so many rules and regulations about sales and exchanges that you wonder if they really want to be bothered to sell you anything at all."

Why not think about ways to "go all in" to express gratitude to your customers. Start a gratitude monitor and have team members bring in examples of five ways that companies have creatively said thank you to their customers. Use these to kick off your own brandstorming session about devising ways that are meaningful to your customers. Decide to try 12 new ways to express your appreciation over the next 12 months. Your customers will thank you!

⫸ Elves and cows

Does your brand lend itself to zaniness? Why not? Perhaps this is the year to try some thing outrageous. Or if you're very nervous, something like *calculated* outrageousness! What do you have to lose? Maybe like OfficeMax or Chick-fil-A, you'll have just started a four- or five-year frolicking tradition!

⫸ Personal is universal

Put on A.G. Lafley's hat and observe what bugs your customers (or get them to tell you) about your two pivotal moments of truth. That is, the pre-decision to use your product or service and the actual use of the product or service. What of these concerns are seemingly so personal and specific (like scratchy tee-shirt tags) that you think your brand just might be able to address in a universal way? How can your brand show more compassion for your customers' dilemmas?

9

Kindle Your Inner Amish

I STARTED LIFE as a Jersey girl, but when I was 13 my family moved to Lancaster, Pennsylvania, better known as Amish Country. If you close your eyes I'm sure you can picture it: rolling hills of well-manicured fertile pasture land, black horse-drawn buggies moving slowly along the back roads, colorful Amish clothes blowing in the wind on clotheslines, hundred-year-old farmhouses and tidy barns dotting the landscape. You might even be able to smell the cows. The Amish live "plain and simple" lives, purposefully and respectfully separate from the "English."

There are many days when I crave being Amish. Order, structure, simplicity, limited choices, community, and slowness are in stark and sometimes painful contrast to our modern way of life. I know I am not alone. There are Slow Food and Slow Travel and Slow Christmas movements, Voluntary Simplicity groups, "Enough is Enough" and "Less is More" bumper stickers, Financial Peace University programs, Not-So-Big housing plans, *Real Simple* and *Country Living* magazines, and countless blogs and websites that reflect Amish-like values. Simple pastimes like sewing, canning, knitting and raising your own vegetables are "in" these days. There is even an organization called Project Laundry List to encourage people to hang their clothes out to dry to save on electric bills. Perhaps the Amish are onto something.

According to a *Wall Street Journal* article, "the U.S. Amish population has more than doubled in the past 18 years, growing to about 233,000." While this growing group is small in number, its influential lifestyle is profound. The Amish school shooting that made national headlines in 2006 was noteworthy because of the compassion and forgiveness that the Amish community had towards the killer and his family. The world watched in amazement. Perhaps because of my time living near and around the Amish, they have always held a place of high interest and deep respect in my life. Jay Lehman, founder of multi-channel retailer Lehman's, started a business in 1955 to serve the Amish. This is his philosophy: "My idea was to preserve the past for future generations. My goal has always been to provide authentic historical products for those looking for a simpler way of life." According to his website, "From his Amish customers, Jay learned that non-electric products give us the ability to complete a task faster and more efficiently than commonly accepted modern methods."

This is counter to our usual way of multi-tasking thinking and doing. A recent post on a Lancaster County blog showed pictures of an Amish barn raising after a fire. In six days, a new barn had been framed and a roof was half finished. After two more days you would never have guessed that there had been a fire at all. The blogger asked, "How long do you think it would take government bureaucracy to accomplish what these Amish did in six days?" I'm afraid to ask how long this would take in the corporate world with RFPs, budget proposals, HR hiring practices, and so forth.

Glenda R. Ervin, vice president of marketing for Lehman's, tells us a homespun story about the brand and her dad, Jay Lehman. "When it came to branding for us, we looked at the one thing we have that no competitor could ever poach: Jay Lehman. He is an iconic figure (and luckily for us, quite photogenic). We created a multi-channel presence with his image. Now when he walks through the store, he is greeted by amazed whispers of, 'There

he is…is that him?' He signs catalogs
and gets his picture taken with fans
nearly every day. We also created
what I fondly refer to as 'Flat Dad'
in two locations of the store. They
are full-size photos of him, so when
he isn't there, people can still 'meet'
him and have their picture taken
with him."

Together is better

Stephen Covey, author of *The 7 Habits of Highly Effective People*
and founder of the Covey Leadership Center, merged his company with Franklin Day Planners in 1997 to form Franklin Covey.
Today, its motto is simply "We enable greatness." Covey has always
been a proponent of creative collaboration and working synergisti-
cally. This is exactly what he describes as Habit #6: interdependence, being better together. The Amish would say it's the secret
to their highly efficient, super fast barn construction. All hands
on deck. Everyone working towards a common goal. Acting like
a beachball.

Being better together starts with simple things like actually
knowing your co-workers, spending time with them, valuing their
expertise, and thinking about your customers first and foremost;
not acting independently and getting bogged down in turf wars.
As a company, we need to think and act more like a beachball.
Yes, independently we are smart marketers and merchants and
financiers, but how might our interdependence make us smarter
together?

In the days before Twitter, Facebook, and all the other always-
on and always-alluring social media technologies, *Megatrends*
author John Naisbitt wrote about our need to counterbalance

"high tech" with "high touch." I spend a great deal of my time with companies helping them connect to the "high touch" aspects of their brand—that is, their inner Amishness. It's a back-to-basics approach. I find that brands need constant reminders to connect and relate, to simplify, to go low tech and to build barns.

Only connect

It is hard to imagine the Amish tweeting or texting one another. They are believers in face-to-face contact. Call me old fashioned, but I still believe that the most fruitful business exchanges happen in person.

Recently American Airlines ran an ad with this headline: "Eye Contact. Your Most Underrated Skill Set." The copy reads, "Sometimes, the more business you do face-to-face, the more business actually gets done."

The Capital Grille, a national upscale steakhouse, shares this same philosophy in one of its full-page ads: "You are cordially invited to cancel lunch with your laptop and broker a deal over something truly wireless. Namely, a white tablecloth, dry aged Porterhouses and single malt scotch. Let's reinstate the three hour lunch, stop using blackberry as a verb and do business eye-to-eye." As a brand, it wants to help its customers "wine, dine and dazzle" their customers.

The first thing I do in my brand work is to get brand leaders to connect in person. I ask them to turn off their BlackBerries, leave their cubicles, and just sit around the same table together and try not to work in fragments for just a day. This is no small feat but I've found that seven or eight hours of a little human connectedness can go a long way. Many times I hear people say that they never knew what a fellow employee did just a few cubicles away. Most have never gathered together interdepartmentally to mull over a particular topic in depth. As mentioned earlier, I call these "Stop and Think days" and we do just that, all day, sometimes two!

It isn't easy. This is new behavior for most people used to jumping from one screen to another, texting during meetings, and generally just not being very present to the person or subject at hand. Our multi-tasking and general lack of concentrated attention is hurting our brands. *BusinessWeek* verified this in a recent article on the costs of distractedness. "It's official: the average knowledge worker has the attention span of a sparrow. Roughly once every three minutes, typical cubicle dwellers set aside whatever they're doing and start something else—anything else. It could be answering the phone, checking email, responding to an instant message, clicking over to YouTube, or posting something amusing on Facebook. Constant interruptions are the Achilles heel of the information economy in the U.S. These distractions consume as much as 28 percent of the average U.S. worker's day, including recovery time, and sap productivity to the tune of $650 billion a year, according to Basex, a business research company in New York City." Ah, and to think that the Amish somehow make do without electricity! We need to unplug every once in awhile and connect face-to-face.

Sometimes I start off these meetings by asking people to make a list of five things that bring them joy. And, I invite those who want to share something from their list to do so in a round robin fashion. There's no pressure, of course but most want to share. "Taking my daughter fishing." "Reading mystery novels." "Running." "A clean house." "Mountain biking." "Meals homecooked by someone else." "Poker." "Bubble baths with the door locked for half an hour." These joy lists begin our connection points for the day. They are "little reveals" that help humanize the people sitting next to each other or down the hall or at the other end of cross-country virtual meetings. They give us a glimpse into our colleagues' passions outside of the workplace and provide fodder for future connections and conversations. Without a human connection, we tend to think of people as cogs in a corporate machine and relate to them one dimensionally, if at all. We never get behind their name badges or their titles.

This is especially true as it relates to our customers. We connect with them only as potential money-makers for our brands—past, present, and future consumers of our products or services. We tend to think of customers as mere demographic data points: working women aged 35 to 55, or Gen Xers, or SOHO owners, or even worse, as mentioned in Chapter 8, target audiences or eyeballs or wallets or giving units. When did we lose sight that first and foremost our customers are complicated human beings just like us? That they are as time-pressed as we are? That they appreciate a good deal just like we do? That they might be juggling sick kids, elderly parents, travel schedules, mortgages, and college payments like we are? That their lives are as full and demanding and hectic as ours? Have you ever thought to ask your customers what brings them joy?

One company tapped into the humanness of its customers in a very deep way. Dove, the beauty brand owned by Unilever, not only sought to put a real face on its customers for internal branding purposes, but it actually used the real faces of its customers in an external ad campaign. Years ago, Dove started a campaign called Real Beauty, where it asked customers of all shapes, sizes, and colors to be its models. This strategy has been more effective than any glitzy, million-dollar, top name model-driven campaign could ever have been. Real Beauty has become a successful and purposeful self-esteem platform for Dove. It has launched Mother/Daughter Self-Esteem Guides, a Uniquely ME! Workshop series, and a Dove Self-Esteem Fund "developed to help free the next generation from self-limiting beauty stereotypes" and to "promote a wider definition of beauty." More recently, Dove ran a TV campaign entitled "Let your beauty sing" where women reveal their perceptions of their beauty flaws openly and honestly. Dove has put a very human face on its brand strategy and has inspired many other brands to do the same.

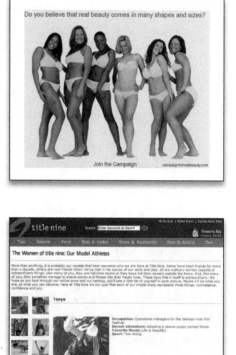

I am seeing more and more brands put real people in their advertisements and in their multi-channel communication materials. Missy Parks, founder of Title Nine does a brilliant job of this. She knows what brings her customers joy. Title Nine showcases its model athletes throughout its catalog and website with mini-snippets of their personalities described in brief fashion like this:

> Rachel
> Occupation: Labor and delivery nurse
> Passion: Dance

and

> Anona
> Occupation: Water Resources Planner
> Talent: Dinner in less than 10 minutes

Parks discusses this on the Title Nine website:

"It is probably our models that best represent who we are here at Title Nine. All are ordinary women capable of extraordinary things. Like many of you, they are full-time moms or they have full-time careers outside the home. And, like many of you, they somehow manage to weave sports and fitness into their hectic lives. These days that in itself is extraordinary. We hope as you look through our online store and our catalog, you'll see a little bit of yourself in each picture. Here at Title Nine it's our goal that each of our model shots represents three things: competence, confidence and joy."

Über high-tech brand, BlackBerry, ran a campaign asking real customers why they loved their BlackBerries. Short and sweet and to the point. Says customer R.T. Fitch, "My work takes me everywhere you can imagine, but my heart is always on my ranch in Houston. My BlackBerry keeps me connected and close to home." Another customer, Crystal McCray Anthony, said, "I'm a mother, novelist, producer and TV commentator. Whether I'm reading an email from my children's school about a snow day, or sending comments on a script to my producing partner, my BlackBerry smartphone keeps me in touch and on track." Customers tell it like it is and by sharing, put a human face on the brand. Like Title Nine, BlackBerry wants potential new users to "see a little of themselves" in each ad.

Franklin Covey, experts in training, consulting, and planning products, knows that one of the many benefits of its planning tools is to help business people have more time for their personal lives. It, too, incorporates real customers in its multi-channel campaigns. Here are two examples:

Aaron Jordin, (pictured in his bike gear) a director of operational services in his business life has this to say about his personal life:

I am a volunteer cycling coach.

I am a recovering ice-cream addict

I am a nurturing dad

I am a planner

Or, attorney Stephanie Hoggan (pictured exercising in an outdoors park):

I am a wannabe football coach.

I am a braised ribs lover.

I am a budding scrapbooker.

I encourage brands to learn about their customers' passions, connect their brands to those in some way, and watch how their brands get exalted in their customers' eyes. Try it!

Becoming more human as a brand strategy may sound obvious but think about your last several business transactions. Was there anything human about them? How much face-to-face or eye contact did you really have? Even if you were in a retail store with another person handling your transaction, was he or she truly connecting with you? Or like many of my frustrating experiences, was she ringing up your sale while also on the phone or robotically telling you to have a nice day? Did she know much about the product you just purchased or show any enthusiasm? Did he thank you for your business? Did he seem to care at all? I don't see a lot of companies capitalizing on the personal touch, the warm connection. Brands need help becoming more human.

Some companies like Edward Jones, Chase, and Paramount Books (publishing company of this book) take pride in their "human factor." It's become a key differentiator these days. They believe in connecting with their customers personally, not via

"inbox by inbox." "No voicemail here. Customer service by real people is our forté," says Doris Walsh, president of Paramount. Bobbi Brown, founder of the eponymous cosmetic company, was quoted in *The New York Times* as saying: "I don't email people. I call them because I want them to hear my voice. I just think people need to hear people's voices, and it takes a second. I don't want to have an email relationship. I just think that something is lost."

I am not a Luddite. As all the social media attest, human connectivity can happen virtually. I applaud the companies that make this a priority. It takes extra work and intentionality to create community. The King Arthur Flour Company, an employee-owned company headquartered in Vermont, prides itself on this: "From Maine to Hawaii, our customers feel that they have a personal relationship with King Arthur. They have incredible loyalty to us and our products, not to mention a sincere enthusiasm that is constantly generating additional customers. Many bakers consider a visit to our store in Vermont a veritable pilgrimage." How does King Arthur do this? Besides its friendly and knowledgeable staff of bakers, it fully immerses its customers in all things bread with The Baking Education Center, Baker's Store, Baking Sheet newsletter, and of course, its very own Bakery.

Is your brand a veritable pilgrimage?

The gift of simplicity

"Simple Gifts"

'Tis the gift to be simple, 'tis the gift to be free,
'Tis the gift to come down where we ought to be . . .

—Elder Joseph Brackett, 1848

This Shaker song gets to the heart of another way to bring out your brand's inner Amishness: the gift of simplicity. Again, look at some of the most successful brands today and a high-touch core value for most of them is simplicity. It's what they *don't* have or what they're not *doing* that sets them apart. Google has brought a virtual library into every home. Unlike most websites, it does not have a busy home page. Google's iconic clean white screen gets its customers where they need to go quickly and easily. Amazon's one-click shopping "and then it's done" philosophy helps customers check one more thing off their lists. It does not make its customers navigate the website in order to check out. Zappos simplifies its customers' entire shopping experience and entices them with free shipping both ways (orders and returns). As new economy companies, Google, Amazon, and Zappos do a good job of remembering the old economy value of simplicity.

James Avery Jewelry shares a similar approach:

"We are in the connection and meaning business, not just the jewelry business 'sharing life, love and faith through the beauty of design.'" From James Avery himself, "I do not consider myself a jeweler as the name implies today. Rather, I like to think of myself as an artist presently concentrating in the precious metal media. I think the creative problems in designing jewelry are the same in any design field, but with the wearability dimension added. I strive to keep designs from being contrived, cluttered, or cute. The challenge is to keep things simple."

Other marketers have created entire brands around their "inner Amishness" and nostalgic values of simple living, handmade and homespun gifts, practical tools, and old-fashioned comfort food.

Gooseberry Patch, a charming collection of country-inspired gifts and home décor, was started over 25 years ago when next door neighbors JoAnn Martin and Vickie Hutchins started chatting about the things that brought them joy. Their shared passion for "all things country" launched Gooseberry Patch, a "Country Store in a Mailbox" (and now online and in stores) and built a loyal following of like-minded customers. In a recent chat with Liz Plotnick-Snay, the company's chief operating officer, she told me, "The brand continues to evolve. Our customers just can't get enough of our cookbooks. So in response to that demand, we are refocusing our business on being a cookbook publisher! Our customers have always been social types but we found out just how social when in just four short months, we are already in the top two percentile of corporate pages on Facebook!"

Lehman's also understands the power of today's social media environment. Glenda R. Ervin, vice president of marketing for Lehman's explained, "We are very active in social media, using high tech to sell low tech. Given his druthers, Dad (Jay Lehman) would have nothing to do with Facebook, YouTube, Twitter, etc. But you know what? It's not about him. It's about the customer. And that's where they are, particularly the young people. We need this younger demographic because those over 80 remember our product line, but they are no longer adding to their possessions. So how do I make a wringer washer or butter churn appealing to a 30-year-old professional? Explain how, why, and where to use it. People care about three things right now: a) the economy b) the environment and c) what they eat. So we make our 'old' products viable in this 'new' world."

The Orton family, self-described "frugal Yankees," started Vermont Country Store more than 60 years ago. As "purveyors of the practical and hard-to-find," the Ortons continue to build a business in partnership with their customers. They invite customers to request "product comebacks" and these memory triggers have helped their merchants find Kewpie dolls, silver tinsel Christmas decorations, and vintage candies and perfumes.

In addition, Vermont Country Store goes beyond the typical "100% Satisfaction Guarantee" that most companies use and posts what they call a "Customer Bill of Rights":

The Vermont Country Store
PURVEYORS OF THE PRACTICAL AND HARD-TO-FIND

Live Help   ▸ View Basket

Catalogue Quick Shop | Customer Service | Gift Cards | Order Status

New This Spring   Apothecary   Apparel   Food & Candy   For The Home   Toys   Yankee Bargains

In the News
Product Videos
The Orton Family Point of View
Customer Service
  100% Guarantee
  Contact Us
  Customer Bill of Rights
  Email Signup
  Live Help
  Order Status
  Privacy & Security
  Questions/FAQs
  Request a Catalogue
  Returns & Exchanges
  Shipping Information
  Site Map

Customer Bill Of Rights

1. To expect polite, courteous service.
2. To be the top priority of the moment.
3. To expect all salespeople to know about their merchandise.
4. To complain about any shortcomings in merchandise, service or delivery.
5. To compliment superior quality of service and merchandise.
6. To expect The Vermont Country Store to stand behind its merchandise.
7. To expect any adjustments in merchandise to be made in the most convenient manner.
8. To expect accurate and efficient record keeping, despite the computer or other problems.
9. 100% guaranteed satisfaction. We will exchange any item or refund your money, without hassle or fuss.

I especially like number 2: *To be the top priority of the moment.* What a refreshingly simple but courteous way to treat customers! Vermont Country Store knows that while its customers may long for the simpler days of the past, they are very much living in our fast-paced, time-crunched present. It has made its online-shopping experience "simpler, easier and better."

A little further south is another company whose mission is to "Please people. Nothing more. Nothing less." That's Cracker Barrel's simplifying corporate goal and it's the motivation behind everything it does. Originally started as a place that travelers could trust when they were on the road, CEO Mike Woodhouse says that

40 years later, it's still all about trust. In an interview in *Nation's Restaurant News,* Woodhouse said, "It centers around trust. What you see is what you get from us. We're never going to surprise our guests in a negative way, never going to have anything but an open, honest presentation of ourselves." With revenues of almost $2 billion, Cracker Barrel does not spend a lot of time on its own rocking chairs. Rather, it works hard to continue to find both big and little ways to please its customers. With so many inquiries about its antique décor (all authentic items you'd find in an old country store), Cracker Barrel dedicated an educational section on its website to sharing its antique expertise with its customers. At Cracker Barrel, its simple but real "Please people" strategy has taken it far.

Deb Downing, founder of Gotta Love It, a gourmet food company, knows all about the power of simplicity and pleasing people. People either love her main ingredient—garlic—or they don't—it's that simple. Says Downing, "When I was branding the first product in my company—which happens to be a garlic butter product, I tried to get the consumers attention by describing exactly what qualities the customer would need to want to buy my product. Since garlic is the main ingredient, and my butter is loaded with it, I call my product "Gotta' Love Garlic!" That way the consumer knows exactly what kind of commitment they need to make before purchasing my product—they better LOVE garlic! There are so many decisions to be made at the food stores these days . . . I wanted to keep things simple for my customer. This product also simplifies their lives as it has many purposes and can help make an ordinary meal extraordinary in no time.

"So, when brainstorming a brand name for my bakery—which specializes in one-of-a-kind hand-decorated cut-out cookies—I wanted to convey the same kind of 'you gotta love this product to buy it' idea. I quickly discovered that when a customer would pick up a box of my cookies, they'd open the lid and inevitably I'd hear 'I LOVE IT!' So I call my bakery the "Love It Bakery!"—a bakery with a personal touch."

How good a job does your brand do in pleasing your people?

Go low tech

Creativity experts talk about the unique connections that can happen when you use the opposite hand to write or scroll your mouse. I believe the same thing can happen when we unplug from electronics and pull out chalkboards, white boards, yellow pads, markers, and sticky notes. Business leaders such as Virgin CEO Richard Branson and Microsoft chairman Bill Gates use low-tech methods like these for creative thinking. So do I.

I see low-tech signals everywhere in the "English" world. Whether it's the return of vinyl albums for the younger generation or the 30 percent increase in the sales of canning supplies, the surge in gardening, sewing, and knitting, brands that tap into their customers' desires to counterbalance the highly complicated tech world we live in with high-touch activities will endear themselves to their customers. "Old school" brands that have been around for 75 + years like Crayola and LEGO have always been low-tech superstars. They've learned ways to become a bit ambidextrous. Both these brands have learned how to successfully combine the best of both worlds. For example, Crayola has online art exhibits and interactive play for children, while LEGO unveiled WeDo, an educational product that links the child's physical and virtual worlds.

Still, the joy of low tech remains. Etsy, a worldwide community of artisans started in 2005, ranked number 44 in *Fast Company's* list of the world's most innovative companies with over $181 million in sales in 2009. Esty's vision is "to build a new economy and present a better choice: Buy, Sell and Live Handmade." This online gathering of craftspeople encourages the personal interaction and artist involvement that customers have come to love at weekend local arts and crafts shows. Their low-tech product sales continue to increase as artists now have a worldwide outlet for their wares.

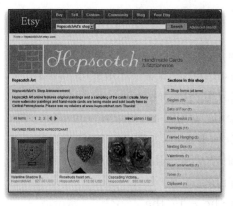

Renee Reese, artist and owner of Hopscotch Art, told me this about her Etsy experience: "The Etsy community is united by a passionate need to share our hand-made creations. We make our art, in my case, watercolors and hand-crafted greeting cards, photograph them and post them online. Part of the fun is marketing your own wares by writing catchy descriptions and providing lots of photos of each item. You want the potential buyer to almost be able to feel and touch the product, so you spend the extra time to craft your web page. Within Etsy, we form teams united by a common material used or geographic area. I can click 'Shop Local' and check out all the other 'Etsians' here in Hershey, Pennsylvania. I can also post, blog, compliment and share crafty ideas with the Etsy Paper Team whose commonality is 'paper lovers!' On the team site, we really feel the love as we comment on each other's new postings, mostly with compliments and lots of exclamation points. It feeds our artists' souls! Basically, within Etsy we are grateful for the love and attention we feel even through what could be an impersonal cyberspace."

How ambidextrous is your brand?

Second acts

Thriftiness is an Amish virtue. In today's tumultuous economic times, being frugal serves us all well. Another area where my outsider-insider role has proved valuable for my clients is in helping them "look in their product attics" and rediscover some priceless gems that might be worth a second look. Is your company sitting on an unmined goldmine of product investment? Almost every company I know has a wealth of potential new product ideas right in its very own closet of past merchandise. The "past" can be as recent as last season, three years ago, or further back to your company's founding, or even outside your industry altogether. I like to call this closet a merchketeer's Plan R: R for repurposing, R for rethinking, R for reimagining, R for reinventing and even R for reviving. Plan R is all about a product's second act.

In his latest book, *Outliers: The Story of Success,* Malcolm Gladwell reminds us "Sometimes constraints actually create success." Our depression-raised grandparents knew this too. Forcing yourself to work with what you have can be good for both the bottom line and for tapping into the right side of your brain. How creative can you be?

Plan R reminds merchketeers to bring forth the richness and the robustness of the past. Fashion and home designers are doing it all the time as they reinterpret clothes or furnishings from times gone by and apply contemporary new twists. Candy companies have had a field day in recent years as they have colorized and "holidayized" what once were season-specific candy to *every* season (Did you see the snowman marshmallows or the orange and black jelly beans?) Movies, musicals, songs, and even some books all have revivals.

At some point in time, merchketeers invested in art, copy, design, samples, manufacturing dies, and prototypes for these original products. Many of these new products became success stories and in due course, were picked up and carried again over the seasons and eventually retired. By reimagining these "retired" products in new ways, merchants can give these winners a second act. Here are a few practical ideas.

Repurpose

Steve Leveen, co-founder of Levenger, shared one of the best repurposing stories I know at a conference on merchandising where we presented together. For years, one of Levenger's iconic products has been a lap desk. Steve reminded us that one of the very first lap desks was designed by Thomas Jefferson for drafting the Declaration of Independence. Levenger's original kidney-shaped reproduction was crafted out of high-quality cherry veneer. This lap desk then spurred the idea for the Laprador Leather Lap Desk, a smaller lap desk complete with a multifunctional pull-out drawer, that better suits the needs of working with a laptop computer. Steve then found himself in a surf shop looking for a surfboard for his son. The surfboard material—lightweight, yet sturdy and smooth—spurred the idea for a Surf Desk. After many iterations, Steve repurposed a surf board into a beautiful new product for customers who "enjoy its lighthearted functionality." Repurposing can indeed be fun.

Reimagine

I first experienced the power of reimagining a product more than 20 years ago while working as a merchant for a book and gift boutique in Old Town Alexandria, Virginia. In those days, books were sold and shelved vertically with other books, plain and simple. These were the days before Amazon and Starbucks cafés in Barnes and Noble bookstores. In my role as the book buyer, I collaborated with the gift buyer to create unique displays that featured books as they might appear in our customers' upscale homes. Coffee table books resting on end tables with decorative lamps or candles nearby. Cookbooks on kitchen shelves with imported gourmet food nearby. Books helped promote the gifts and home accessories we were selling and vice versa. Just look at any Pottery Barn catalog spread or Anthropologie store layout. Imaginative cross-selling works and even helps some products have an unplanned second act.

Reimagining can be as easy as reassigning places or positions for your products.

Nancy L. Schneider, director of merchandising for Cooking Enthusiast, recounted this experience: "Our new merchandising strategies are prompting us to dig deeply into our pool of past products as a source for items that tie directly into a cultural theme or recipe. While I don't recommend chasing truly bad performers (a dog is a dog), we have been successful turning marginal items into winners by taking a fresh approach to how they are merchandised. For example, we've been selling French snails along with the shells and serving pieces for an authentic escargot presentation. When the snails were featured in a recipe (Escargot & Porcini Mushrooms in Brandy Cream Sauce) our unit sales almost doubled."

Repackage

The publishing world is masterful at repackaging "content" into calendars, gift books, serials, movie tie-ins, and events (from the *Chicken Soup* book series to the Harry Potter enterprise). Gail Richards, creative director for Whizbang! Creative, knows the value of reformulating content. "A whole new world of possibilities opens up when people realize the many ways in which their intellectual capital can be turned into products. From tangible products like card decks, games, or audio, to service products like teleclasses, there are literally countless ways to package what you know. And when you do that, you build your core business and your brand in the process."

Boat and Tote Bags

L.L.Bean is often my premier example of creative line extension. The boat tote, one of its iconic products, has been masterfully reconfigured in numerous ways (shapes, sizes, stripes, colors). But my favorite repurposing idea is the way it repackaged a mini tote into a seasonal gift container. The small canvas tote now has become a clever (and practical) holder of a Down East Blueberry Breakfast gift, a Dog Treat gift, or even an amaryllis-filled tote at the holidays.

In what ways might your best-selling products be repackaged into new products?

Revive

Some companies make a business out of reviving products. Think vintage clothing stores, classic cars, or eBay or even The Vermont Country Store, a brand that specializes in the "practical and hard-to-find." For more than 60 years, Vermont Country Store has built a business bringing customers items that they have long remembered and missed. Jane Patton, head of merchandising for this old-fashioned brand says, "We focus on what we have always done . . . practical frugality with a touch of nostalgia. It is our practice to always bring back 'revivals' (what we call products from the past)." On its website, Vermont Country Store encourages its customers to reminisce about products from the past, whether memories of a candy counter, Fisher-Price toys, or even Lifebuoy soap.

How can you revive products from your past?

Business strategist Alexander Kandybin, writing in *MIT Sloan Management Review,* reminds us that "Product development is not a business for those who are afraid to start over." The potential savings gained by the ingenuity of your company's PLAN R, might be just the competitive advantage you need to survive today's lean economic times. Don't be afraid of the R word!

Kindle Your Inner Amish Homework

So, with inspiration from the Amish, why not set aside some time to try these exercises with your brand leaders.

⫸ Casting call

Superstars Harrison Ford and Kelly McGillis starred in the Amish movie, *The Witness,* but companies like Dove, Title Nine, Franklin Covey, and Under Armour, the performance athletic brand, did a casting call for non-celebrity, real users

of their products. Why not adapt this idea to your brand and do a casting call of your own? Recruit customers to send a recent photo of themselves and ask them to tell you five things that bring them joy with two being somehow related to your product or services. See what you discover! Perhaps this will indeed lead your brand to launch an ad campaign based on this knowledge or simply serve to round out your one-dimensional view of your customers—not a bad outcome in and of itself.

⫸ Barn raising

Forget those ropes courses and contrived business bonding exercises and get to work building something meaningful together as a team. This could be something to benefit your customers, your company, or your community. Just do it!

⫸ Simplify! Simplify!

Another frugal Yankee, author and naturalist Henry David Thoreau, cautions us to take simplicity seriously whether for the sake of our lives or our brands. "Our life is frittered away by detail. Simplify, simplify." How can your brand do a better job of giving your customers the gift of simplicity?

Integrate Dreams

I KNOW I should no longer be surprised when a Venn diagram of my life interests—spirituality, business innovation, and writing—intersect, but I still am. Recently I was listening to Richard Rohr, founder of the Center for Action and Contemplation, teach on the topic of non-dual thinking. Like Susan Scott of Fierce, Inc., he, too, is convinced of the immense power of the small word "and." Here's an abbreviated excerpt from what Rohr sees as a few of the benefits from seeing things with what he calls a "non-dual mind."

The Shining Word "And"

"And" teaches us to say yes

"And" allows both–and

"And" keeps us from either–or

"And" is willing to wait for insight and integration

"And" keeps us inclusive

"And" allows us to critique both sides of things

"And" allows us to enjoy both sides of things

"And" allows us to be both distinct and yet united

Soon after I absorbed Rohr's spiritual work, Roger Martin's book *The Opposable Mind: Winning through Integrative Thinking* crossed my desk. After reading this, I wanted to introduce the two men.

Similar messages, different spheres of influence. Martin defines integrative thinking as "the ability to face constructively the tension of opposing ideas and, instead of choosing one at the expense of the other, generate a creative resolution of the tension in the form of a new idea that contains elements of the opposing ideas but is superior to each." He writes, "The most common failing of conventional thinking is the tendency to lose sight of the whole decision. It may be easier to dole out pieces of a decision to various corporate functions, but that ensures that no one will take a holistic view of a particular problem. And in the absence of a holistic view, a mediocre result is the likely outcome."

I see and experience brand mediocrity all the time. I'm sure you do too. Brands settle for "good enough" outcomes while their customers crave being wowed. Brands need integrative thinkers. Brands need leaders who take holistic approaches to all their strategic decisions. They need to model that behavior throughout their organizations so that we have apprentice integrative thinkers in line for the next round of leadership opportunities and brand dreams.

"I'm not an either-or kind of guy," A.G. Lafley told Roger Martin while he was still the CEO of P&G. Martin writes, "The results of thinking in terms of 'and' rather than 'or' have been breathtaking. Lafley has led P&G to consistently strong organic revenue growth, double digit profit growth and a doubling of the company's stock price within four years. In doing this, Lafley has established himself as one of the finest CEOs of his era."

What's your Lafley factor? Are you making more either-or decisions than you'd like? Have these been good for the brand? Perhaps it's time for an 'and' mindset shift so you can bring some progressive non-dual thinking to your present brand dilemmas.

Steve Jobs, CEO of Apple is another integrative thinker. *Fortune* quotes Jobs as saying, "We're the only company that owns the whole widget—the hardware, the software, and the operating system. We can take full responsibility for the user experience. We can do things the other guy can't." Apple is a fully integrated beachball brand.

Not all companies need or want to be fully integrated vertically, but they certainly might have room for more "horizontal" integration throughout their organizations. Brands have work to do in this regard. Brands have lessons to learn from integrative thinkers—people like Richard Swensen (margin) and Gawande (checklists). If brand leaders' thinking and strategizing is not integrative, their actions and execution will not be either.

But before any of this can happen, sometimes we first have to do some shedding.

SHED

I learned this term "shed" from the queen of organizing, Julie Morgenstern. Here's how she describes it: "SHED is a practical process for decluttering your life to make room for change. SHED can help you clear out the old in your life to make room for the new. It is an acronym for the steps to letting things go:

Separate the Treasures,
Heave the Rest,
Embrace Your Identity and
Drive Yourself Forward.

Substitute the word "brand" for "life" and you'll understand the connection. It is fair to say we all have a place either in our homes or offices that we hope others won't see. Whether it's the crammed closet, the toss-it-all-in-here-who-really-cares junk drawer, or the overstuffed three-car-garage or the musty attic boxes and the sagging basement shelves, we all have some place that just doesn't pass Martha Stewart muster. These places don't look like those perfect Pottery Barn or Container Store catalog spreads (thus the reason they are called *aspirational*) no matter what bins or functional-yet-decorative shelves we buy. We have just accumulated too much stuff.

Many Americans are feeling overextended, overstuffed, and overspent. Although we seem to be feeling the effects more recently, it isn't a new problem. Back in 1986, comedian George Carlin told us we all had too much stuff. In his monologue on "stuff," he reminded us, "A house is just a pile of stuff with a cover on it. You can see that when you're taking off in an airplane. You look down; you see everybody's got a little pile of stuff. All the little piles of stuff. . . . Sometimes you gotta move, gotta get a bigger house. Why? No room for your stuff anymore. Did you ever notice when you go to somebody else's house, you never quite feel a hundred percent at home? You know why? No room for *your* stuff! Somebody else's stuff is all over the place . . ."

Well, if our homes or offices can accumulate too much stuff over time, so can our brands. Brands can suffer from a case of *avoirdupois,* a word describing a heaviness and a ponderousness, a burden. We pile on more and more business activities. At times our various departments go off in conflicting directions; our channels get promotion heavy and our profit potential gets bogged down with "good" stuff, but perhaps not the best. We know that focusing on doing good things is indeed the enemy of doing what is truly the best, but we keep doing good. Good is easier than best. Good habits are hard to break.

So what are we to do? How do we air out our brands and see what we've got in our brand attic, closets, junk drawers, and garages that no longer works for us or for our customers?

Is it time you conduct an internal brand rummage sale? Eric Harvey, president of Walk the Talk, and his co-writer Steve Venture comment, "Our brains are like closets. Over time they are filled with things we no longer use—things that don't fit. Every once in awhile they need to be cleaned out." I suggest brands and the people who manage and create them schedule a brand review and clean up day. And soon!

Prepare for these cleanup days just like you would if you were having one at your own home and yes, you have to include the boss. A.G. Lafley understood his main role to "be one of deciding what business they [P&G] are in and what business they are not in." It is a lot of work hauling out all that junk and facing bad decisions, irrelevancy, and places where the brand overspent needlessly, totally missed the mark, or forgot to get its customers' opinions on crucial decisions of impact to them. But ask people who have had a successful garage sale recently and one of the joys they describe is letting go of all the past mistakes and saying goodbye to all the things that kept them feeling, well, rather *avoirdupois*! The things you've had to work around. The misunderstandings. The confusion. The brand clutter. The irrelevancy of certain communication materials, of procedures that are outmoded.

Perhaps you'll even uncover some sacred brand cows that get broken in the moving and reviewing process. Management expert Peter Drucker counsels, "It's easier for companies to come up with new ideas than to let go of old ones." Letting go is what a rummage sale is all about. All the physical and emotional energy around this activity will help your brand move from good to best.

Just when you are tired and think you've had enough, I encourage you to keep going. Get all the way to the back of the brand attic. Just like when you helped your grandma clean out her cluttered spaces years ago, you are likely to uncover some real brand treasures back there, some valuables that you might have overlooked or forgotten that were buried in the chaos. Things like one-of-a-kind brand "antiques" such as the owners' original passion or the founder's original dream, glimmers of useful ideas that were not acted upon, or customer suggestions that fell through the cracks but now appear to be spot-on for implementation. Clean spaces invite possibilities, clearer thinking, and new beginnings. Oh, the joy of seeing things from a fresh and roomy perspective!

Brand rummage sales are more than a way to shed some avoirdupois. They are also cathartic. They have the potential to free brands and their creators from what is holding them back, draining their energy, taking them off focus. These brand cleaning and cleansing days encourage us to change our ways, to make "stop doing" lists alongside of all the "start doing" lists we have. They help us close doors. They help us become more intentional editors, strategic questioners, and energy collaborators. The benefits of the fierce conversations that occur around all of these topics can help brands leap forward into new vistas unencumbered.

Jim Collins is a serious practitioner of intentional editing. He has his own version of my purple colander. According to a profile of him and his latest work in *The New York Times,* he is able to produce such meaningful books on management and leadership because he purposely focuses his time on just three main tasks. By ruthlessly editing out all the activities that don't align with those three goals, he is able to marshal his energy for the very best. How many tasks are you juggling as a brand leader? Which ones might you have to say "no" to in order to say a more full "yes" in other areas?

Roll up your sleeves, get a little dusty and dirty, and work hard lugging the old stuff out. Take time to reminisce and savor the once forgotten treasures. Toss all that is irrelevant. Toss more. Let go of the past mistakes. Then stand back. Look at the clean space. Breathe. Smile. Make George Carlin and your customers happy that you paid attention. Hopefully, you've got less stuff. And hopefully, it's nothing but the *best* stuff!

Now, back to the beachball

So now that your brand has some breathing room and margin and clean spaces, you'll start to see things a bit more clearly. When you look across your marketing channels, do you smile as you see a version of your brand's very best or does it look more like brand pandemonium? If you don't see either of these extremes, do you see something between ho-hum or, even worse, something similar to what all your competitors are doing? Just exactly what brand story is being told across all your channels? And, more importantly, what story is it that your customers are seeing and feeling and reading between the lines of all your merchandising and marketing activities? Is it a comprehensive and logical narrative or a collection of random and disorganized pages?

If we asked customers these questions, I don't think we'd like their answers. According to *Internet Retailer*, customers think there is a lot of room for improvement. Here are a few recent headlines: "Retailers still have work to do in cross-channel strategies" and "Consumers find crossing the channel frustrating." *Internet Retailer* cited a Forrester Research, Inc. study that showed that consumers are most happy when they buy products in one channel, but are somewhat frustrated when they do research online and then make purchases with a traditional retailer. Brands must pay attention to this. This is not beachball behavior.

This is important because *McKinsey Quarterly* reminds us, "Consumers who shop across a number of channels—physical stores, the Internet, and catalogs—spend about *four* times more annually than those who shop in just one. Companies that get multichannel retailing right can enjoy larger profit margins and yearly revenue growth more than 100 basis points higher than companies that don't. The kind of multichannel retailing that fuels sustainable growth and margin expansion requires a tightly integrated strategy across all channels. Each channel needs to play a clear (and often quite distinct) role in supporting and reinforcing a retailer's overall brand equity."

Creating an integrated channel experience for your customers starts with your brand story. Brand stories provide the basis for that holistic approach as well as a strategic and defining narrative for both your internal and external audiences. Without a brand story as a true north compass for all your strategic business activities, your brand can lose its soul. Without making that story clear to your customers in all that you do, your brand can lose its competitive edge.

Brand stories also inspire a rich merchandising milieu. Creative merchketeers enrich the brand narrative by developing persuasive product experiences for their customers. They do this not just by selecting or creating on-brand items, but by infusing those items with relevant meaning. In our BrandAbout way of seeing across industries, let's see what we can learn from these examples.

Books & Books

Mitchell Kaplan has always been on a mission—to create community through book love. His independent bookstores in South Florida and the Caribbean are heaven on earth for book aficionados. By hosting 70 diverse author events a month, Kaplan connects his customers' passions (art, design, architecture, fashion, regional

literature) with products (books and unusual gifts) and provides an atmosphere that encourages purposeful lingering in the stores' den-like stacks and shelves as well as the cafes. Kaplan and his well-read staff befriend their customers, becoming knowledgeable about their reading habits and interests. They care. They connect. They share like minds.

Kaplan's brand story started organically over 27 years ago but continues to be a story that involves community, books and devotion. Whether you connect with this brand through one of its many poetry readings or community gatherings or online or in one of its brick and mortar stores, you are enveloped by an integrated, thoughtful and memorable literary experience that keeps you coming back for more.

Vineyard Vines

Started by two brothers in 1998, this nautical clothing company knows that the art of storytelling and the sport of sailing go hand in hand. Vineyard Vines (VV), best known for preppy clothes and men's ties, does an excellent job of creating an integrated and interesting brand experience across all its channels. As the inspiration for all their new products, founders Shep and Ian Murray feature beautiful East Coast wooden boats on catalog pages. And, they playfully encourage stretching sailing season out as long as possible: "You heard it here first: Columbus Day is the new Labor Day."

They've incorporated photos of real sailors wearing Vineyard Vines products and their mini-stories about sailing adventures. In all three channels, it is apparent that Shep and Ian live the brand. Their customers are their sailing friends and their sailing friends are their customers! In VV's retail channel, stores are designed in nautical white and blue paint and accented in wood trim and sail-

ing decor. Their website boasts a "Whale of a Sale" and features their iconic whale logo products for serious and not-so-serious sailors alike. VV's story is one of subtly encouraging "The Real Good Life" at every brand touchpoint.

Bass Pro Shops

Bass Pro's story is all about being the world's leading supplier of premium outdoor gear and giving people "more outdoors for their money." Its stores have become tourist attractions. A recent news article boasts that they have more visitors than Walt Disney World in Orlando and the stores are billed as being as "close to the Great Outdoors as you can get indoors!" Its website offers an OutdoorSite Library as well as another customer-driven Outdoor Answers area, both full of practical tips and product suggestions for its community of outdoor enthusiasts. Value is a predominant theme in headlines, sale offerings, and price comparisons. A gold star marks Bass Pro-branded items ranging from sophisticated sports equipment to pink and traditional camouflage motif Christmas stockings for younger outdoor enthusiasts. The Bass Pro catalogs are thick wish books geared to sportsmen's dreams, including the world's first "fish-ready" professionally rigged boats. All of these products are fed by the passion of Johnny Morris, the entrepreneurial CEO who also sees his role as "Chief Day Dreamer." He lives the brand and is passionate about all aspects of the Bass Pro story.

Serena & Lily

I love watching companies grow and evolve. In just five short years, Serena Dugan and Lily Kanter have made heads turn in the product categories of nurseries, baby clothes, and now, master bedrooms. Self-described as "two go-getter Type A scatterbrains," they've followed their hearts and passions into creating Serena &

Lily, a brand that resonates with "gypsy moms" and others who "make it up as you go." "You never know what you might find" is the thread of their newest story, Bazaar, an eclectic collection of "treasures that make our rooms and yours one of a kind." Their catalog and website are full of original product creations (Market Slings, Sausalito Baskets), creative new twists on others you've seen before (Letter Pillows, Personalized Dishes for children), and options for those artsy customers who like to create their very own décor (headboards, upholstery). Working mothers and business owners, Dugan and Kanter understand their customers' full and frenzied lives and their ever-changing needs. By living the brand and evolving with their customers, Serena & Lily's story has become a book that their customers just can't put down.

LEGO

For some, LEGO lust begins early. For others, it never stops. LEGO's name means "play well" and its website touts that "it has come a long way over the past 70 years—from a small carpenter's workshop to a modern, global enterprise that is now,

in terms of sales, the world's sixth-largest manufacturer of toys." While thought of primarily as a children's toy brand, LEGO also has a loyal following of adults. A recent "Invent the Future" contest was open to both kids and adults. LEGO's brand story is all about "learning through play" and its channels provide visual and practical reinforcement of this narrative. The theme of its annual magazine called *The Brick* is "Let the Children Play" and it provides a deeper glance into the brand and all its worldwide activities. If you haven't experienced LEGO since your childhood, it's time to look again. Product categories are as diverse as action figures, robotics, watches, and complex customized items. Two customer-driven programs, LEGO Ambassadors and LEGO Certified Professionals keep this brand's story relevant and providing what one analyst called "many hours of repeatable joy."

Take a time out and look again across all your channels, closely and with new eyes. Get some of your customers involved. Be hard on yourself: is your brand story as clear, creative, and compelling as it could be? Is it a voila! experience across all your channels? An integrated and engaging brand experience takes intentionality, persistence, and a bit of "and!" It's a must-do.

Dreaming and doing

The examples above show us that the important work of brand harmony is an all-hands-on-deck, everyday assignment. But every so often, brand leaders need to pull back, get away from the nitty-gritty, day-to-day, and do some dreaming. I've always been inspired by these words of Sarah Ban Breathnach: "The world needs dreamers and the world needs doers. But above all, the world needs dreamers who do." She captures the necessity of moving between the worlds of doing and dreaming. She is an integrative thinker.

Many of my clients make dreaming a regular branding practice. Group, an innovative church ministry resource company, has what it calls "Dream Days." Amy Nappa, executive editor and champion for women's ministry at Group, loves everything about the word dream. "I love that it conjures up 'might thinking' as in . . . 'we might do this, we might do that.' I love that dreaming allows us to let go of our daily distractions and think long term. I love that it always leads to new endeavors for our company from product ideas like a new book offering to wider options like partnerships. A Dream Day is exactly how our new (and now worldwide) Girlfriend's Unlimited ministry came about. It all started with a dream!" (And I love that Nappa has the word Champion in her title. Another great brand practice!)

Great brands never stop dreaming, no matter the size or strength they achieve. General Electric was named by *Forbes* as the world's largest company in 2009. Jeff Immelt, GE's CEO, talked about some of his growth processes for the company in *Strategy + Business:* "We host 'customer dreaming sessions' to drive innovation. These one-to-two day sessions are held at the company's John F. Welch Leadership Development Center with the CEOs and key leaders from the GE businesses."

No matter the size of your company, the industry you are in, the products or services you provide, dreaming is a must-do. Even Disney, a beloved brand that lives the word "dream" and uses it throughout its brand charter, from selling dreams, to its tagline "Where dreams come true," to the newest ship in its cruise line fleet "Disney Dream," never stops dreaming. *Women's Wear Daily* describes Disney's latest dream as ". . . creating a coast-to-coast retail sequel stretching from Southern California to Times Square. . . . The new concept will feature an assortment of Disney products; interactive displays for children using Disney characters and themes (a 'magic mirror' is one such element); theme park-style attractions like a 'princess castle' in the store and a children's theatre with customized viewing material, such as movie clips from Disney's recent releases."

What is your brand dreaming about these days?

Victor Hugo prompts, "There is nothing like a dream to create the future." But as we all know, brand dreams need passionate integrative thinkers and leaders to make them come true. In *The*

Opposable Mind, Martin writes, "Bruce Mau, a renowned designer and frequent collaborator with architect Frank Gehry, told him, 'You can't become a renaissance person anymore, because the range of what you would need to do is just impossible. But you could actually assemble a renaissance team.'" I like that idea.

Does your brand have an RDT (Renaissance Dream Team) already? Or might you need to conduct a BrandAbout assessment of your present team's passion, emotional intelligence, integrative thinking, doing and dreaming potential? Might some stretch assignments get you where you want to be? Might some customers need to be part of that team?

Imagine just what might happen if this Renaissance Dream Team tossed around that beachball and played in the brand for awhile!

Integrate Dreams Homework

Practice! Practice! Practice!

⫸ Ruminating after the rummage sale

Conducting a brand rummage sale can be exhausting, but it can also be quite freeing. Take a look at all the things, ideas, and dreams that your brand decided to shed. Go and celebrate your clean brand over a round of drinks. Talk about what it meant to shed some of those practices and possibilities. Toast the closed doors as well as the new open space! As Jeffrey Phillips, VP, sales and marketing for OVO Innovation found, "Closing doors by clearly defining your strategic goals is even more important than opening them."

⫸ Potential reviews

I first learned about the concept of "potential reviews" from a roundtable conversation that *McKinsey Quarterly* published in 2009 on the subject of "Navigating the New Normal." Rik

Geiersbach, chief strategy officer of Boeing, said his company now has "potential reviews," which evaluate whether the assumptions in its planning process still hold. Geiersbach's original intent had to do with business plans. But why not borrow that brilliance and conduct a potential review with your team members as it relates to assembling a Renaissance Dream Team for your brand. How many opposable minds do we have? Who needs a stretch assignment? Who needs coaching on "and"? And who might just need a newly redefined integrative merchketeer position?

⫸ Dream lists

Walt Disney once said, "If you can dream it, you can do it. Always remember that this whole thing was started with a dream and a mouse." Today, this is how The Walt Disney Company he founded in 1923 is described: "Together with its subsidiaries and affiliates, Disney is a leading diversified international family entertainment and media enterprise with five business segments: media networks, parks and resorts, studio entertainment, interactive media and consumer products. Disney is a Dow 30 company with revenues of approximately $36 billion in its most recent fiscal year." From one little mouse to $36 billion in less than 90 years. Not bad!

Schedule your own brand Dream Day. List your dreams. Dare to dream big.

PS

Afterword

WHEN DEAN AND I sailed in the South Pacific we met an incredibly interesting couple named Dieter Dyck and his wife Senikau. As a child, Dieter had survived Hitler's nightmare and had a dream to move as far away from Germany as possible. A few years later, he took a ship across the world to New Zealand and there met Senikau, a German-Tongan woman. They fell in love, married, raised a family and built a business in New Zealand. The business faltered due to New Zealand's recession in the 1980s, so they packed their family and moved to Senikau's homeland of Tonga, a remote, tropical island in the South Seas and started all over again building another business, The Tongan Beach Resort. Dean and I and our sailing mates had the privilege of being their guests a few years ago one Christmas. It was our most memorable holiday ever as adults. In the candlelight on Christmas Eve, along with four other guests and Dieter and Senikau, we all sang "Silent Night" in our native languages and then we read the Christmas narrative in the Gospel of Luke. This holy tête-à-tête was one of many long conversations we had with Dieter about life, about business, about spiritual practices. It was our own private walkabout of sorts. We came away deeply moved. This South Pacific pause gave us much to mull over. Dieter quietly mentored us about the things that matter most.

I thought a lot about Dieter and Senikau as I wrote this book. About how intentional they were in putting all these BrandAbout verbs into action as they created a restful respite for their guests. About how they had a dream to create a tropical haven for travelers and how that dream was not a wishful "someday" bucket list thing but was a real tangible plan that they worked towards against many odds (Dieter tells their story in his memoir, *A South Sea Dream Come True*. After 25 years of running the resort, Deiter and Senikau have retired and now their daughter and son care for the business.). About how he didn't let failure get in his way. About how he befriended his customers—truly and meaningfully. And about how he crafted a playful and restful experience for his guests that would be "remembered for life."

Play. Be. Listen. Conduct. Dare. Herald. Craft. Reveal. Kindle. Integrate. Ten powerfully important verbs that will transform your brand and your product offering if you are intentional about putting them into action. Please don't let this be a book that sits on your shelf. Read it, yes. But use it. Share it with your team. Dog ear the pages. Act on the exercises. Develop your own. Create margin in your daily business schedule to make these verbs come alive as part of your on-going brand practices.

I hope these BrandAbout practices will inspire you to go on your own version of a business walkabout. To look up and out and all around your brand and how it intersects with your customers' lives. To find meaningful ways to connect the soul of your brand with your customers' expressed and unexpressed needs and desires. To rediscover the passion that started your brand story and to put these practices into motion—playfully, joyfully and intentionally!

Here's your permission slip!!!

Selected Bibliography

Ackerman, Diane. *Deep Play*. New York: Vintage, 2000.

Benioff, Marc. *Behind the Cloud: The Untold Story of How Salesforce. com Went from Idea to Billion-Dollar Company—and Revolutionized an Industry*. San Francisco: Jossey-Bass, 2009.

Branson, Richard. *Business Stripped Bare: Adventures of a Global Entrepreneur*. London:Virgin Books, 2010.

Brown, Stuart. *Play: How it Shapes the Brain, Opens the Imagination and Invigorates the Soul*. New York: Avery, 2009.

Cameron, Julia. *The Complete Artist's Way: Creativity as a Spiritual Practice*. New York: Tarcher/Penguin, 2007.

Chouinard, Yvon. *Let My People Go Surfing: The Education of a Reluctant Businessman*. New York: Penguin, 2006.

Collins, Jim. *Good to Great: Why Some Companies Make the Leap . . . and Others Don't*. New York: Harper Business, 2001.

————. *How The Mighty Fall: and Why Some Companies Never Give in*. Boulder: Jim Collins, 2009.

Covey, Stephen. *The 7 Habits of Highly Effective People*. New York: Free Press, 2004.

Crawford, Matthew. *Shop Class as Soulcraft*. New York: Penguin Press HC, 2009.

Csikszentmihalyi, Mihaly. *Flow: The Psychology of Optimal Experience*. New York: Harper Perennial Modern Classics, 2008.

De Pree, Max, and Walter C. Wright Jr. *Mentoring: Two Voices,* (monograph), Pasadena: Max De Pree Center for Leadership, undated.

Gawande, Atul. *The Checklist Manifesto: How to Get Things Done Right.* New York: Metropolitan Books, 2009.

Gill, Michael Gates. *How Starbucks Saved My Life: A Son of Privilege Learns to Live Like Everyone Else.* New York: Gotham, 2008.

Gladwell, Malcolm. *Outliers: The Story of Success.* New York: Little, Brown and Company, 2008.

Lamott, Anne. *Bird by Bird: Some Instructions on the Writing Life.* New York: Anchor, 1995.

Martin, Roger. *The Opposable Mind: Winning Through Integrative Thinking.* Boston: Harvard Business Press, 2009.

May, Matthew E. *In Pursuit of Elegance: Why the Best Ideas Have Something Missing.* New York: Broadway Books, 2009.

McLaren, Brian. *Finding Our Way Again: The Return of the Ancient Practices.* Nashville: Thomas Nelson, 2008.

Mooney, Kelly. *The O.P.E.N. Brand: When Push Comes to Pull in a Web-Made World.* Berkeley: Peachpit Press, 2008.

Naisbitt, John. *Megatrends: Ten New Directions Transforming Our Lives.* New York: Grand Central Publishing, 1988.

Quinlan, Mary Lou. *Time Off for Good Behavior: How Hardworking Women Can Take a Break and Change Their Lives.* New York: Broadway, 2005.

Rath, Tom and Barry Conchie. *Strengths-Based Leadership.* Washington, D.C.: Gallup, 2009.

Reichheld, Frederick. *The Ultimate Question: Driving Good Profits and True Growth.* Boston: Harvard Business School Press, 2006.

Sawyer, Keith. *Group Genius: The Creative Power of Collaboration.* New York: Basic Books, 2008.

Scott, Susan. *Fierce Conversations: Achieving Success at Work and Life One Conversation at a Time.* New York: Berkley Trade, 2004.

Silverstein, Michael J. *Treasure Hunt: Inside the Mind of the New Consumer.* New York: Portfolio, 2006.

Swensen, Richard A. *Margin: Restoring Emotional, Physical, Financial, and Time Reserves to Overloaded Lives.* Colorado Springs: Nav-Press, 2004.

Tharp, Twila. *The Creative Habit: Learn It and Use It for Life.* New York: Simon & Schuster, 2005.

Tickle, Phyllis (editor). *The Ancient Practices Series.* Nashville: Thomas Nelson, 2008–2010.

Trout, Jack. *Positioning: The Battle for Your Mind.* New York: McGraw-Hill, 2000.

————. *Repositioning: Marketing in an Era of Competition, Change and Crisis.* New York: McGraw-Hill, 2009

Ueland, Brenda. *If You Want to Write: A Book About Art, Independence, and Spirit.* Minneapolis: Graywolf Press, 1987.

Index

About the Author

Andrea Syverson is a customer-centric listener, connector, and creator. As a right- *and* left-brained creative marketing strategist with over 25 years experience, she holds the customer in highest regard in all decision-making processes.

By actively and intuitively listening to customers, she has created and developed best-selling products and strategies across a variety of categories—from gifts and stationery and books to gourmet food and apparel to spirituality, and many in between. Her clients include many large and small giants: Hallmark, Hershey Foods, Ben & Jerry's, Celestial Seasonings, Spanx, Boston Proper, Compassion International, and World Vision, just to name a few. While she holds an MBA, Andrea acknowledges that her true expertise comes from continuous hands-on customer experiences.

Syverson loves her work as a brand provocateur. She's helped companies "stop and think" about their product positioning, their brand relevance, their customer needs. She's helped companies get back to the heart and soul of their mission, reposition themselves if necessary, construct product and brand fit charts, creatively brainstorm the future and develop strategic merchandising and marketing plans that place their customers' needs first and center. Her clients appreciate her warm and enthusiastic style and ability to work as an "outsider-insider."

She is president of IER Partners (*www.ierpartners.com*), a national consulting firm based in the Rocky Mountains, specializing in branding, strategic planning, merchandising, new product development and creative thinking. She may be reached at *asyverson@ierpartners.com*.